# BRAND IDENTITY

**Brand Identity**

Edited by Sumiwo Hasegawa ©
Published by Graphic-sha Publishing Company Ltd.©


First Edition 1990
ISBN4-7661-0548-6

Graphic-sha Publishing Company Ltd.
1-9-12 Kudan-kita Chiyoda-ku Tokyo 102 Japan
Phone 03-263-4318
Fax 03-5275-3579
Telex J29877 Graphic

Printed in Japan by Toppan Printing Co., Ltd.

# ロゴONパッケージ

長谷川純雄編

グラフィック社

# はじめに

日曜日の午後などに，家の者と連れだってストアに買物に行くのが私は好きだ。荷物持ちを兼ねて食品や雑貨のあふれる売場をゆっくり歩きながら，デザインウォッチングを楽しむ。新しく発売された商品が目に入ると，甘いお菓子であろうと婦人用品であろうと手に取って見る。そしてパッケージのデザインとロゴタイプに素早く，注意深く眼を注ぐ。評価し，記憶しながら歩く。斬新なデザインと出会ったときの気持…他人の見事な仕事に軽く嫉妬しながらも，優れた作品を見たという一種の快感を覚えるということはないだろうか。デザインに引かれて買って来てしまうこともしばしばだ。中身を賞味し，使用した後の空き箱，空き缶を仕事場のあちこちに積み上げて，折りにふれて観察する。

パッケージデザインの幾つかの要件のなかで，最も重要なのはロゴタイプのデザインではないだろうか。広く流通する商品は，そのネーミングと共にロゴタイプの視覚的な面からまず，人々に記憶されるからだ。デザイナーが力を注いで作ったロゴタイプを大きな図版でじっくりと眺め，それが箱や缶や瓶や袋の上で生きて使われている様子を観察し，そのデザインの魅力の秘密を探ってみること，それが本書を編集する動機であり，狙いである。デザインは鑑賞するものではないが，分析し，批評することは無駄ではあるまい。

本書の構成を概観してみる。まず英文のロゴタイプを集めた。オーソドックスなローマン体とサンセリフ，つまりゴシック体を使ったものが大多数を占めることは容易に理解できるだろう。特に後者は，明快で分かり易く，ネガティブにしても可読性に欠けず，細いものから太いものまで，あるいは装飾を加えたり大胆に変形したりして，バリエーションを作り出す可能性の幅が大きいので最も好まれて使われる書体である。頭文字をシンボルにした作品と数字をテーマにしたロゴタイプにもスポットをあててみた。前者は正しくはロゴタイプだとは言えないかもしれないが，切れ味鋭い作品ばかりで楽しいページになったと思う。

日本字のロゴタイプは筆文字によるものが実に面白い。デジタル文字だワープロだと，みんな文字を丁寧に，気持を込めて書かない時代になったというのに，筆文字ロゴタイプは健在である。日常的でないところに魅力があるのだろうか。切り絵，切り文字という技法も日本的な情趣を表現する手段として重宝されている。掲載した137点の一つ一つに，筆者が簡単な紹介や批評や観察を付け加えてみたので目を通していただきたい。

数年にわたって本書の構想を抱きながら取材を続ける間に，どれ程の商品が新しく発売され，そして消えていったことだろうか。いつか話題にしようと手元に収集しておいたのに，いざ掲載という段になって，今はもう販売していないからと，それがかなわなかった商品が幾つも幾つもあるのだ。数々のヒット商品の蔭で，あっという間に消えていったパッケージたちに今も愛着が残る。

収録作品の取材をする過程で，多くの企業の担当部署の方々，デザイナー諸兄の手を煩わしてしまった。しかも紙数に限度もあって，多くの作品を掲載できなかったことをお詫びかたがた，みなさまに厚くお礼申しあげたい。

近頃，使うため食べるために買ってきたどんな小さな箱や袋でも，必ず一度は裏表を眺めてみて，無造作に破って屑籠へ捨てたりできないでいる自分に気が付く。プロ意識の表われと見るか，悲しい習性と自嘲すべきだろうか。

長谷川純雄

# PREFACE

I enjoy shopping with my family on Saturday afternoons. I like to browse and look at the designs of food and household good packages in the various product sections. I also enjoy helping my family carry bags. When I see new products on display, no matter whether they are sweets or products for women, I just grab them and carefully examine their package designs and logos. I browse while evaluating and memorizing them. The feeling when seeing original designs – don't you derive pleasure from seeing splendid works, even while feeling pangs of jealousy because they are not your own? I often purchase things just because the designs are great. After appreciating the contents, I pile up the empty boxes and cans here and there in my office. Later, I occasionally look at them.

I believe that the most important element in a package design is the design of its logo. This is primarily because multifarious products are remembered by their names or through their visual impact. To see the magnified logos that designers concentrated their efforts on with all due care; to see them in actual use on boxes, cans, or bottles; and to study the charms of the designs – these are the reasons for publishing this book. Although graphic designs for advertisement are not for art appreciation, neither is it useless to analyze and comment on such designs.

I will give an outline of the composition of this book. First, I collected logos in which English letters are used. You might easily guess that Roman and sans serif type are used in most of the logos I obtained, that is, Gothic type accounts for more than half the total. Gothic is especially clear and easy to read, even as a negative. Moreover, it can be used in a variety of faces, from very thin to ultrabold; in decorative styles; or in boldly transformed styles. Thus, it is quite popular. I also focus on logos symbolizing the initials of product names and those representing numbers. Although the former cannot properly be called a logo, I think those keen works will contribute to enjoying the book.

Japanese-language logos are particularly interesting in their calligraphy. With the advent of digital characters and word processing, people no longer infuse their feelings into writing. Calligraphic logos still exist, however. Perhaps the fact that they are not an everyday sight is what makes calligraphy so attractive.

Cut out characters are also quite useful in expressing Japanese feelings. I give simple opinions and observations about each of the 137 works printed in the book.

I wonder how many new products were sold, then disappeared during the several years I was gathering data for this book. Some products that I collected to talk about someday were not realized because they were not being sold at the time I became ready to examine them. I am still quite attached to the packages that disappeared, however.

In the process of collecting data about the works to be printed, I was obliged to bother some personnel, such as the designers in charge of relevant departments, in many companies. I am grateful for their patience. I apologize for being unable to print many works due to space limitations. I thank all of them for their support.

Nowadays, I find myself looking at the boxes and bags, even small ones, of products that I purchased to use or eat; and I find myself unable to discard them after use of their contents. Should I think of this as professional pride? The sadness of habit? I wonder.

Sumiwo Hasegawa

# 凡例

CD——クリエイティブディレクター
AD——アートディレクター
D——デザイナー
LD——ロゴタイプデザイナー
PD——パッケージデザイナー
I——イラストレーター
CW——コピーライター
A——エージェント
C——クライアント

CD——Creative Director
AD——Art Director
D——Designer
LD——Logotype Designer
PD——Package Designer
I——Illustrator
CW——Copy Writer
A——Agent
C——Client

**■写真撮影**
表紙, Intermezzo,商品写真47点

**スタジオGT 秋田淳之助**

Photographs by
**Junnosuke Akita**

ロゴONパッケージ
BRAND
GRAPHIC-SHA
BRAND IDENTITY
edited by Sumiwo Hasegawa
GRAPHIC-SHA

KIRIN
DRY

**1**
ドライビール
D—PAOS
C—キリンビール
1990

ブームを呼んだドライビールも，少しずつ品質を変えながら第2世代に移り，販売戦略の変化にともなってロゴタイプもデザインが変ってきた。極太のオプチマを使いモダンなセンスで売ったキリンドライビールも，90年に入って，コーポレートロゴタイプであるKIRINの書体にイメージを合わせた古典的なローマン体に変わり，格調高い雰囲気をもつに至った。100年の歴史をもつ麒麟のキャラクターが，今日的なアルミ缶の冷たい地肌にもマッチして，リッチなムードを醸し出しているのも素晴らしい。

**1**
Beer
D—PAOS
C—Kirin Brewery Co., Ltd.
1990

The dry beer boom has entered its second generation with gradual changes in quality. KIRIN's logo has also changed with changing sales strategies. The style of the lettering of today's KIRIN Dry beer has changed to classical Roman letters conforming to the image of KIRIN's corporate logo for the 90s. KIRIN's 100 year-old characters create a rich mood perfectly suited to the cold surface of modern aluminum cans.

**2**
コンパクトディスク
D—河島 彰
C—ファンハウス
1988

さわやかなキャラクターで人気のシンガーソングライター，岡村孝子のヒットアルバムSOLEIL＝ソレイユのタイトルである。
両端のSとLを大きくする着想は他にもいくつか例があるが，このSOLEILは最も成功した一例だと思う。縦太のローマン体の力強さをソフトな中間色でカバーして品の良い仕上りとなった。
バラの花を背景にしたデザインが明るく美しくて岡村のキャラクターにピッタリだ。裏面も同様にきれいな仕上りなので一緒にお見せしよう。

**2**
Compact Disc
D—Akira Kawashima
C—Fun House
1988

SOLEIL is the title of a hit album by Takako Okamura, a popular singer-songwriter with a refreshing personality. I believe SOLEIL to be one of the most successful titles in that both ends, S and L, have been vividly conceptualized. The power of long, thick Roman letters neutralized by soft, intermediate colors provides a refined finish to the album.

LIBERA
MILDS

**3**
たばこ
AD—田中 晋
D—都坂政彦
C—日本たばこ
1987

LIBELAはLIBELAL＝自由の意味。オーソドックスなローマン体で，特別に変った書体を使っているわけではないが，一字一字の線の太さ，字の間隔や角度などに行き届いた配慮を十分感じさせる，完成度の高いロゴタイプである。両端のLとAを大きくしたところが魅力のポイントで，LからIへ，RからAへのつながりが自然で美しい。

**3**
Cigarette
AD—Susumu Tanaka
D—Masahiko Tosaka
C—Japan Tobacco Inc.
1987

LIBERA means LIBERAL, or, free. Orthodox Roman letters are used; no special lettering is used. Each letter's thickness, intervals between letters, and letter angles have been carefully considered and represent a finely finished logo. The L and the A at the ends are larger than other letters and the connection between the L and I and the R and A seem natural, even beautiful.

# KIRIN FINE PILSNER

**4**
ビール
D—PAOS
C—キリンビール
1989

コーポレートロゴタイプKIRINの書体をそのまま展開して，社名と商品名とに一体感をもたせたロゴタイプである。Lで変化をつけて字組みが冗長になるのを上手に避け，しかものびのびとした表情をもったデザインである。PILSNERとは，チェコの地方都市ピルゼンで生まれたビールの製法に由来している。

**4**
Beer
D—PAOS
C—Kirin Brewery Co., Ltd.
1989

This logo has developed naturally from the lettering of the KIRIN corporate logo. It gives a sense of unity to the company name and product name. A twist has been given to the L and wordiness in the letter combination has been avoided, resulting in a relaxed design. Pilsner is derived from a beer brewing method originating in the Pilzen region of Czechoslovakia.

5
缶コーヒー
AD—橋本近雄・麻布デザイン
D—菊地 学
C—キリンビール
1987

他社にさきがけて缶コーヒーのシリーズ化に成功してヒット商品となったJiveは，図のような基本ロゴタイプを使用するものに限っても現在8種類を数える。
黒と赤で統一した太目のローマン体はオーソドックス過ぎるくらいだが，ミルクが入ってマイルドになるに従って豆の色と缶の地色が少しずつ変化し，品質感をよく伝えている。

5
Canned Coffee
AD—Chikao Hashimoto, Azabu Design
D—Manabu Kikuchi
C—Kirin Brewery Co., Ltd.
1987

Jive, a first among hit products in the canned coffee series, presently consists of 8 kinds of coffee, in spite of its basic logo. The standardized thick red and black Roman lettering is rather too orthodox, but as milk is added to present a milder image, the color of the beans and the can gradually change, clearly representing quality.

6
チューブ入り味噌
AD—U.G.サトー
D—平良勝彦
C—玉松味噌醤油
1989

日本の味〈味噌〉といった先入観をきれいさっぱりと取り去った外袋のデザインが新鮮である。扱いが簡便で汚れないチューブ入り味噌の清潔感がよく表われている白い袋もさることながら，英文表記に徹して，サン・ローラン風でさえある黒と金の文字組みによる大胆なロゴタイプが異彩を放っている。DASHIIRIとはかつおや貝柱の出し汁入りという意味。玉松味噌醤油は，仙台を中心にシェアをもつ宮城県のメーカーである。

6
Miso (Bean Paste)
AD—U.G. Sato
D—Katsuhiko Taira
C—Tamamatsu Miso-Shoyu Co., Ltd.
1989

This fresh outer design completely removes the stereotypical "taste" of Japan. The white container expresses the ease of use and cleanliness of tube miso. Greater still is the accent on the English with its radical lettering resembling the red and gold lettering of St. Laurent. DASHIIRE means a soup stock of dried bonito shellfish muscles. Tamamatsu Miso-Shoyu is a manufacturer in Miyagi prefecture with shares centered around Sendai.

DASHIIRI
MISO

**7**
キャンデー
CD—明治製菓
AD—星野健三
LD—星野健三
PD—星野健三・藤本 泰
I—高村太木
C—スシャール・トブラー
1986

このごろは珍しくなった缶入りのフルーツキャンデーである。手にもてばカラカラと懐かしいドロップの音がする。CRESTとは最高という意味か。内容をシンボライズしたワッペン風の装飾をともなった繊細なタイポグラフィ・デザインである。イラストの部分も含めて色彩に透明感があり，良い意味での作りものの美しさに引かれるものがある。

**7**
Candy
CD—Meiji Seika
AD—Kenzo Hoshino
LD—Kenzo Hoshino
PD—Kenzo Hoshino, Yasushi Fujimoto
I—Taiki Takamura
C—Suchard Tobler
1986

This is a rare canned candy which has recently reappeared. Held in one's hand and shaken, the can makes a nostalgic sound. CREST means the best of something. This is a delicate typographical design with an emblem-like decoration which symbolizes the content. The coloring including the illustration offers a sense of transparency, lending an attractiveness to the artificial beauty in a good sense.

**8**
レギュラーコーヒー
AD—北山 聰
D—徳田三枝
AD—L.D.ファクトリー
C—日本エム・ジェー・ピー
1989

真っ黒のボディに深紅のラインがまず目を引きつける。カメラかオーディオ機器のような重厚感である。本来は黒子である発音記号をそのまま主役にもってきた発想の逆転が，さらに人を引きつける。それもそのはず，[ʃú:tər]はshooter=撃つ人，射手。MIND ʃú:tər=人の心を射るもの。一度飲んだらこのコーヒーの味はあなたの心をとらえて離さない，という訳だ。いつまでも市場に生き残っていてほしい美しいデザインである。

**8**
Coffee
AD—Satoshi Kitayama
D—Mie Tokuda
A—L.D. Factory
C—MJB Japan Ltd.
1989

The eye falls first on the contrast between the red lines and black body. There is a heaviness as with cameras or audio equipment. The reverse idea which places the phonetic pronunciation in the main role as opposed to relegating it to its usual place backstage is especially attractive. Of course, a "shooter" is a hunter. A "mind shooter" is that which grasps the human heart. The meaning here is that once tasted, the heart is taken with this coffee. This is a design which meant to leaves an everlasting impression in the market.

**9**
紅茶
CD—大門敏彦
AD—加藤芳夫
D—藤田 隆
A—Uデザイン事務所
C—サントリー
1989

好みの多様化に備えて種類を豊富にそろえ，容量も各種用意して見事に需要に応えたという点では，サントリーの紅茶シリーズTESSがトップではないだろうか。ここでお見せする以外にも容量の異なるものがいくつかある。
女性の名前Teresaの愛称であるTESS。それにふさわしく金の飾りを身につけて楕円の中に可愛らしくまとめられたTESS。ミルクティーは白く，レモンティーは黄色と，内容に応じて的確に色が変化し，選ぶ楽しみを与えてくれる。

**9**
Black Tea
CD—Toshihiko Okado
AD—Yoshio Kato
D—Takashi Fujita
A—U Design
C—Suntory Ltd.
1989

In terms of arranging many varieties for each person's individual taste, and in terms of a variety of quantities responding to consumer demands, Suntory's TESS tea series is probably ranked at the top. Quantities other than those shown also exist. TESS is a nickname for Teresa. It is neatly placed in an oval with a gold curved line background appropriate to the name TESS. Milk tea is white and lemon tea is yellow, according to the content making the act of choosing itself enjoyable.

**10**
ワイン，ミネラルウォーター
D—大高 猛
C—神戸ワイナリー（ワイン），
神戸市（ミネラルウォーター）
1984

神戸市が地方行政の一環として販売しているワインとミネラルウォーターである。直線的なKOBEの文字と，伸びやかに重なるスクリプト体のWineの文字とのバランスが絶妙で，品の良い，格調高いデザインとなった。WineとWater，共に頭文字にWがきてイメージを統一するのに役立ったのも幸運だったと言えよう。

**10**
Wine, Mineral Water
D—Takeshi Ohtaka
C—Municipal Kobe Winery (Wine),
Kobe City (Mineral Water)
1984

Kobe city sells its own regionally manufactured wine and mineral water. The balance between the straight KOBE letters and the more extended Script lettering of Wine is exquisite, representing a refined and dignified design. The fact that the first letter of both Wine and Water is W helps unify the image.

KOBE
Wine
since 1983

SUNTORY

D·R·Y

SPECIAL

5.5

**11**
ドライビール
AD—川西 明・藤本勝之
D—藤本勝之
C—サントリー
1989

サントリーのドライビールも，缶のデザイン，ロゴタイプともに第2世代である。単なるアクセントとして入れたのかもしれない中黒が，結果的にD，R，Yと文字に区切りをつけることによって言葉を解体して符号化し，さらに無機質な子持ち罫で囲んで，情緒的な要素を一切排除した，まことにハードでドライなデザインである。新たに登場したアルコール度5.5のタイプが，数字に赤い文字を使ったにもかかわらずハードな表情は少しも変化しないで，いよいよ辛口なデザインとなったと言ってよい。

**11**
Beer
AD—Akira Kawanishi, Katsuyuki Fujimoto
D—Katsuyuki Fujimoto
C—Suntory Ltd.
1989

Here we find the can design and logo for the 2nd generation of SUNTORY DRY BEER. The simple accent of black in the center analyzes and symbolizes the word DRY by distinguishing the D, R, and Y. Furthermore, by being surrounded by thick and thin black lines, any atmosphere is completely eradicated, leaving a hard, dry design. And although the numbers of the new 5.5 part alcohol SUNTORY DRY are red, the hard image does not change in the least; in fact, an even drier design can be said to result.

**12**
チョコレート
D—薄井豊子
C—森永製菓
1989

豪華な感じのするチョコレートである。外箱のEXの文字に使われているマーブル模様を中身一つ一つの包み紙全面に使うという凝ったデザイン。それが生クリーム，プラリネの2種類あって，外箱のcream，pralineのところが金箔押しである。菓子類の箱に金箔押しは決して珍しいことではないが，この森永EXはその使い方に軽薄なところがなく，高級感があるのがよい。

**12**
Chocolate
D—Toyoko Usui
C—Morinaga & Co., Ltd.
1989

Here we have a chocolate with a gorgeous' image whose exquisite design
consists of marble print on both the EX on the outer package as well as on each individual inner wrapping. There are two types-cream and praline. Goldleaf has been pressed onto 'cream' and 'praline' on the outside of the package. Goldleaf on boxes of confectionery is not unusual, but this Morinaga EX, is far from a frivolity and presents a rather high class image.

**LEGEND**
**Legend is a dry and light shochu**
**made from choice barley and corn.**
**The flavor and aroma of**
**this special product come alive when**
**enjoyed on the rocks or simply straight up.**

# 宝焼酎
# Legend
レジエンド

**13**
焼酎
AD—宝酒造マーケティング部
LD—人部恭造
PD—人部恭造・金森周一・大泰一晃
A—電通
C—宝酒造
1989

宝焼酎Legendはボトルのデザインからしてウイスキーの雰囲気である。
文字のディテールに一風変った細工のされたLegendを中心に，文字組みのセンスの良さで見せるロゴタイプ全体のデザインもまたウイスキーの雰囲気がある。
"宝焼酎" の文字がなければ見間違えてしまいそうである。それだけ高級感があるということだろうか。アルコールの濃度によって3種類のタイプに分けられるが，25%と35%の違いを，ポジからネガに変身させて見せるテクニックが鮮やかだ。

**13**
Shochu(Liqour)
AD—Takara Shuzo Co., Ltd. Marketing Dept.
LD—Kyozo Hitobe
PD—Kyozo Hitobe, Shuichi Kanamori, Kazuaki Ohata
A—Dentsu Inc.
C—Takara Shuzo Co., Ltd.
1989

At a mere glance, the bottle design of Takara Shochu's Legend presents a whiskey-like impression. With a focus on the uniquely crafted letters, "Legend", the overall design of the logo with its letters smartly arranged also presents a feeling of whiskey. Without the letters "Takara Shochu" one might mistake the product for whiskey. The design can be said to have this much persuasive force. There are 3 types distinguished by their alcohol content.

**14**
紅茶，烏龍茶
P—須藤伸二
AD—原田 進・プラクシス
LD—上野山博志
A—マッキャンエリクソン博報堂
C—日本コカコーラ
1987

街なかの自動販売機で，このブランドを見かけない日はないと言ってもよいくらい，広く親しまれた商品である。SIMBAはつまり神葉。古来から中国で健康に良いとされた茶の葉という意味であろう。デザインのポイントはなんといってもSから伸びる波形のエレメントだ。茶の葉の表現でもあり，また香りが漂い広がっていく様子を表わしてもいる。“神”の字に付けられても全く違和感がないのが見事だ。

**14**
Black Tea, Chinese Tea
P—Shinji Sudo
AD—Susumu Harada, PRAXCIS
LD—Hiroshi Uenoyama
A—McCann-Erickson Hakuhodo Inc.
C—Coca-Cola Japan Co.,Ltd.

One could say that on any given day, these well-known brands are sure to be found in the vending machines of most any city. SIMBA means “holy leaves”, a meaning most likely taken from ancient China for tea leaves considered good for the health. The point of the design is, above all, the wave which extends from the S. In this, we find an expression of tea leaves, and even the presence of the floating aroma of tea. There is no sense of incongruity even with the wave affixed to the word meaning “God”.

NEW
髪に健康、ハチミツのうるおい
髪に毎日やさしい
Timotei
シャンプー・コンディショナー・トリートメント

**15**
洗髪，整髪剤
AD—杉原 稔
D—J.ウォルター・トンプソン・ストックホルム
A—J.ウォルター・トンプソン・ジャパン
C—ニッポンリーバB.V.
1990

シャンプー，ヘアリンス，トリートメントなどの洗髪，整髪料はどのメーカーもいろいろなタイプをそろえて群として店頭で競い合っているが，このtimoteiもその代表的なひとつ。丸味を帯びた柔らかいロゴタイプで親しまれているが，90年に入ってハニー入りのタイプが登場。緑1色だったロゴタイプに黄色が加わって2色刷りとなり一層楽しく華やかになった。

**15**
Shampoo, Hair Conditioners
AD—Minoru Sugihara
D—J. Walter Thonpson Stockholm
A—J. Walter Thonpson Japan Ltd.
C—Nippon Lever B.V.
1990

Any manufacturer of shampoos and hair dressings such as shampoo, hair rinse, treatment, etc., markets a multitude of types arranged in groups at shops for the purpose of competition. Timotei is one such example. Timotei has been well-known for its round, soft logo, but as of 1990, a new Timotei with honey as an ingredient has been added to the market. Thus, to the green logo has been added a yellow one, resulting in a more vivid product representation.

**16**
乳製品
AD—勝岡重夫
D—勝岡重夫・塚田宏子・塩田英明・山田
広宣・倉方康子
C—中沢グループ
1988

中沢乳業を中心とした中沢グループは，1988年にC.I.システムを導入して企業イメージを一新した。明るいブルーと黄のコーポレートカラーによる英文のグループマーク，ブランドピクチャーと呼ぶ農場風景を楕円で囲んだコーポレート・ブランドマーク，この2つを中心にC.I.システムが展開され，製品のパッケージは全てブランドマークで統一されている。

**16**
Dairy Products
AD—Shigeo Katsuoka
D—Shigeo Katsuoka, Hiroko Tsukada, Hideaki Shiota, Hironobu Yamada, Yasuko Kurakata
C—Nakazawa Group
1988

In 1988, the Nakazawa Group centered around Nakazawa Dairy Farms, introduced a C.I. system to refresh their business image. The C.I. system developed by focusing on 2 designs-the English group mark with bright blue and yellow corporate colors, and the corporate brand mark whose 'brand picture' farming scene is contained by an oval. The entire product package is unified by the brand mark.

SUNTORY
モルツ
MALT'S

17
ビール
AD—大森重志
D—柳田美保
C—サントリー
1986

このロゴタイプは，本当はパッケージ全体を囲んでいる黒と銀の子持罫をぬきにしてはその面白さを語れないのかもしれない。この商品の表情というか，不思議な魅力は，囲み罫とロゴタイプの不可分な一体感がつくり出しているものだ。見る者の注意力がぐっと中心に向けられる効果もあって印象を強くしている。

17
Beer
AD—Shigeshi Ohmori
D—Miho Yanagida
C—Suntory Ltd.
1986

This logo might fail to properly present itself without the black and silver lines surrounding the entire package. This product's expression is created by these lines as well as the indivisible unity of the logo. The result is that the observer focuses attention on the center, making for a strong impression.

**18**
たばこ
AD—斎藤陽一
LD, PD—細谷直美
C—日本たばこ
1986

日本たばこではとくにイメージキャラクターとして特定して売り出しているわけではないが，DEANとはジェームス・ディーンを想定したものであろう。
「粋で，過激で，自由で，ちょっぴりユーモラス」という宣伝コピーがその人を想い起こさせるし，なによりもこの，ロスかシスコのネオンサインを思わせる装飾的なロゴタイプが，シネマの黄金時代の再現だからである。

**18**
Cigarette
AD—Yoichi Saito
D—Naomi Hosoya
C—Japan Tobacco Inc.
1986

Japan Tobacco does not sell DEAN as an image character, but rather to prompt recollections of James Dean-cool, violent, free, and somewhat humorous. More than this, however, the decorative logo suggesting the neon signs of Los Angeles or San Francisco represents a reproduction of the heyday of cinema.

**19**
カップ麺
CD—宮地睦明
AD, PD—渡辺 明
LD—田辺慎二
A—博報堂
C—日清食品
1990

間食程度ではなく，本格的な食事になりうる量と内容をもったカップ麺なので，Big China。中華物としてはけばけばしさがなく，俗受けをねらっていない気持ちの良いデザインだ。ロゴタイプのiの点の部分と日清食品のマーク（半円型）のイメージが重なって見えるのは少し深読み過ぎるだろうか。

**19**
Noodle-in-a-cup
CD—Nobuaki Miyaji
AD,PD—Akira Watanabe
LD—Shinji Tanabe
A—Hakuhodo Inc.
C—Nissin Food Products Co., Ltd.
1990

Big China is not an in-between-meal snack, but a noodle-in-a-cup dish with the quantity and content to make it a full meal in itself. As Chinese food designs go, this design is not flashy but comfortable without aiming at popular taste. The dot of the 'i' in the logo and the image of the Nissin mark (semicircle), however, seem to overlap leading one to suppose a deeper meaning or to doubt one's own simple interpretation.

**20**
チョコレート
D―ブルボン・デザイン室
C―ブルボン
1987

ビットと聞けば，今日は誰もがコンピュータの記憶容量の単位のことだと思うはずだ。しかし語源は同じなのだが，食物の一口分という意味がある。ブルボンのチョコレートBitは，この2つの意味を兼ねて表現しているところが巧みである。35ミリ四方の一口チョコをひとつずつ包装して1個売りしている。ロゴタイプも極太書体がひと塊になって1ビットを形づくっている。

**20**
Chocolate
D—Bourbon Corporation Design Room
C—Bourbon Corporation
1987

When you hear 'bit', these days most anyone would recognize it as a unit of memory capacity in a computer. The origin of the word is the same but here it means a morsel, or single mouthful, of food. Thus, Bourbon has skillfully combined the 2 meanings into chocolate bits. These 35 mm square mouthfuls of chocolate are wrapped and sold individually. Even the logo's thick letters seem to create a 'bit'.

Bit

**21**
ドッグフード
AD, PD—大西智津子
LD—日本ペットフード宣伝課
C—日本ペットフード
1987

スーパーストアの食料品売場の一角で見つけたときの印象は非常に新鮮だった。人用の食品の並みのパッケージよりはるかにセンスが良く，明るく，シンプルで清潔感にあふれていた。
ペットフードといえども常に品質改善がなされていて，三度目のリニューアルでnew softとなった。犬の表情の素晴らしさに負けない，カラフルで力強いロゴタイプである。

**21**
Dog Food
AD,PD—Chizuko Onishi
LD—Nippon Pet Food Advertising Department
C—Nippon Pet Food Co., Ltd.
1987

This product's package presented a greater sense, brightness, simplicity, and cleanliness in the food section of a supermarket than did those representing food for people. Of course, this is pet food, but its quality has consistently improved up to its third renewal when it became "new Soft". This logo is colorful and strong, quite representative of the splendor of dogs.

**22**
蛍光灯
D—木村 勝
C—東芝
1987

商品名の頭文字をモチーフにしてシンボルをデザインし，パッケージの主役にしている作品をいくつか続けてご紹介しようと思う。
東芝のサークルライン（円形の蛍光灯）メロウルックシリーズはDaylight, Natural, Whiteの3つのタイプがあり，頭文字D.N.W.とサークルラインを組み合わせたシンボルは，シンプルですがすがしいデザインだ。ダンボールでもこれだけの美しさが表現できるのだ。なかでもNタイプは楕円とNの角度のバランスが安定していて秀逸だ。電気店の店頭でもとび抜けて目につく商品である。

**22**
Fluorescent Light
D—Katsu Kimura
C—Toshiba Corp.
1987

Here follows products whose packages focus mainly on symbols designed by using the first letter of the product name as the motif. There are 3 types in Toshiba's circle line (circular fluorescent light) mellow look series-Daylight, Natural, and White. The sumbol, a combination of the first letter of each word (D,N,W) and the circle, is a simple and refreshing design. The N type is especially excellent owing to the balance between the oval and the angle of the N.

23
清涼飲料水
AD—原田 進・プラクシス
D—渡辺 聡
C—キリンビール
1988

うっかり見過ごしてしまいそうだが，缶全体に描かれたブルーとグリーンの図形がQUARTERの頭文字Qなのである。写真を見て，のどが鳴るような清涼感を覚えるのは，缶からしたたる水滴のためではなく，明快な造形とシンプルな配色の効果なのである。ちなみにQUARTERとは，甘さひかえめ，従来の飲料の1/4という意味だ。

23
Soft Drink
AD—Susumu Harada, PRAXCIS
D—Satoshi Watanabe
C—Kirin Brewery Co., Ltd.
1988

The Q of QUARTER may be completely missed, as its blue or green picture covers the entire can. Looking at the picture, the feeling that one's mouth is watering does not derive from the image of the water droplets but rather from the lucid shape of the Q and the effects of a simple color coordination. Quarter, incidentally, also insinuates a sweetness 1/4 lower than that of conventional drinks.

**24**
化粧品
AD—山下正和
D—池田修一
C—資生堂
1988

シャンプーとリンスの2つの機能をもち，すすぐとリンスに変わるシャンプーなのでリンプーと名付けられた。ここでは頭文字をモチーフにしたシンボルの方をご覧いただくことにする。
太くゆったりとカーブしたrは，乳液の流れる様を連想させたりもして印象的。黒のストライプはヘアラインのイメージか。香りの違いによって2つに色分けされている。

**24**
Cosmetics
AD—Masakazu Yamashita
D—Shuichi Ikeda
C—Shiseido Co., Ltd.
1988

Rinpoo is a shampoo which, when you rinse, turns into a rinse thereby providing a double function. R, the first letter, is the symbol which it is hoped attracts the eye. The fat and gently curved R is impressive in that it encourages you to imagine the way the milky lotion runs. Could the black stripe, then, be an image of the hairline? There are 2 types of Rinpoo, differing in aroma.

**25**
男性化粧品
AD―青木 誠
D―塩沢正秀
C―花王
1987

シャンプー，リンス，ヘアフォームを皮切りに，"男のサクセス"と銘打って登場した花王のSUCCESSは，シンボルとしてのSと英文が一体となって使われる。頭文字をとってシンボルとするとき，サ行音とSの関係ほどわかり易くなじみ易い例はないが，このSUCCESSもその好例と言えよう。ブルーの濃淡でスタートしたシンボルSも，シリーズ商品の多様化で，いろいろなカラーが使われるようになった。

**25**
Men's Cosmetics
AD—Makoto Aoki
D—Masahide Shiozawa
C—Kao Corporation
1987

Kao's SUCCESS for men came out labeled as "Success for Men" beginning with shampoo, rinse, and hair mousse. The symbol S and the English are unified. When taking the first letter of a word as a symbol, there is no easier example of an easy-to-understand symbol than that of the S sound. This SUCCESS is also a good example of this. Starting with a light and dark blue S as the symbol, it has been possible to use various colors owing to diversification of the product series.

**26**
ビデオテープ
CD—植村 徳
AD—高橋 敏
LD, PD—高橋 敏・籠 邦博
C—TDK
1986

TDKのビデオテープ〈SEE〉シリーズが発売されたとき，グレードも収録時間も同じなのにデザインが4種類もあって話題になった。好みのデザインを選択することができるし，録画するジャンルを分類するのにも便利だった。どれも優れたタイポグラフィ・デザインなのでパッケージは全部お見せすることにして，ロゴタイプはシンボリックな"S"1字のもので代表してもらうが，これは筆者の好みでもある。

**26**
Video Tape
CD—Noboru Uemura
AD—Ving Takahashi
LD,PD—Ving Takahashi, Kunihiro Tohshi
C—TDK Corporation
1986

When the TDK video tape SEE series came out, even though the grade and recording time were the same, the creation of 4 different designs became a topic of conversation. You can choose the design of your liking and specify what you will record on them according to the design. Since all four are typographical designs, all have been presented, but the single S is representative as the logo, this writer's favorite.

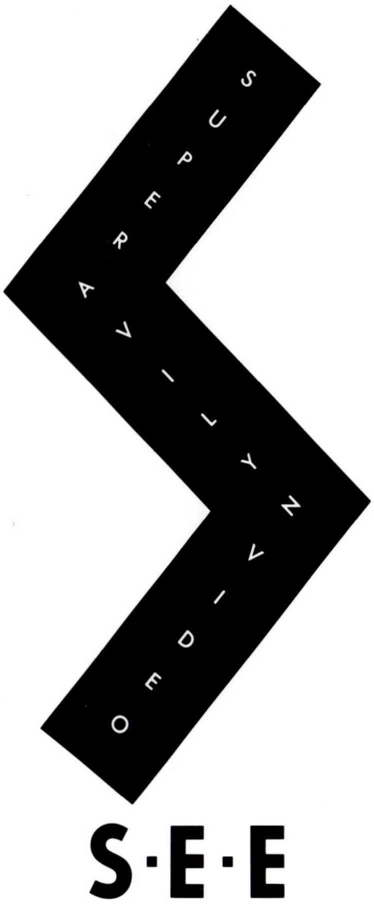

**27**
チョコレート
AD—犬塚達美
D—藤 きみよ・佐藤勝則・藤岡加良子
C—森永製菓
1987

Sをシンボルにした商品は数多くあるが森永チョコレート〈スプーナ〉のように大胆なのも珍しいのではないか。
思い切って上半分をカットし，白地に鮮やかに浮かび上がる赤Sと青S——発売当時はこの2種類だった——その後，このスプーナはヒット商品となっていろいろなタイプが発売されることとなった。
写真左側のデミタイプのように，コーポレートマークと一体になって使われていることが実力の証しであると思う。

**27**
Chocolate
AD—Tatsumi Inuzuka
D—Kimiyo Fuji, Katsunori Sato, Kayoko Fukuoka
C—Morinaga & Co., Ltd.
1987

Many products exist with S as their symbol, but Morinaga's daring chocolate spugna S is perhaps rare. The upper half is cut, with the red S and blue S clearly rising from the white background. These 2 type existed at product release. Later, other various types were developed following the success of these two. As shown in the demi-type at the left of the photo, the fact that the S has become part of the corporate mark illustrates the power of this spugna.

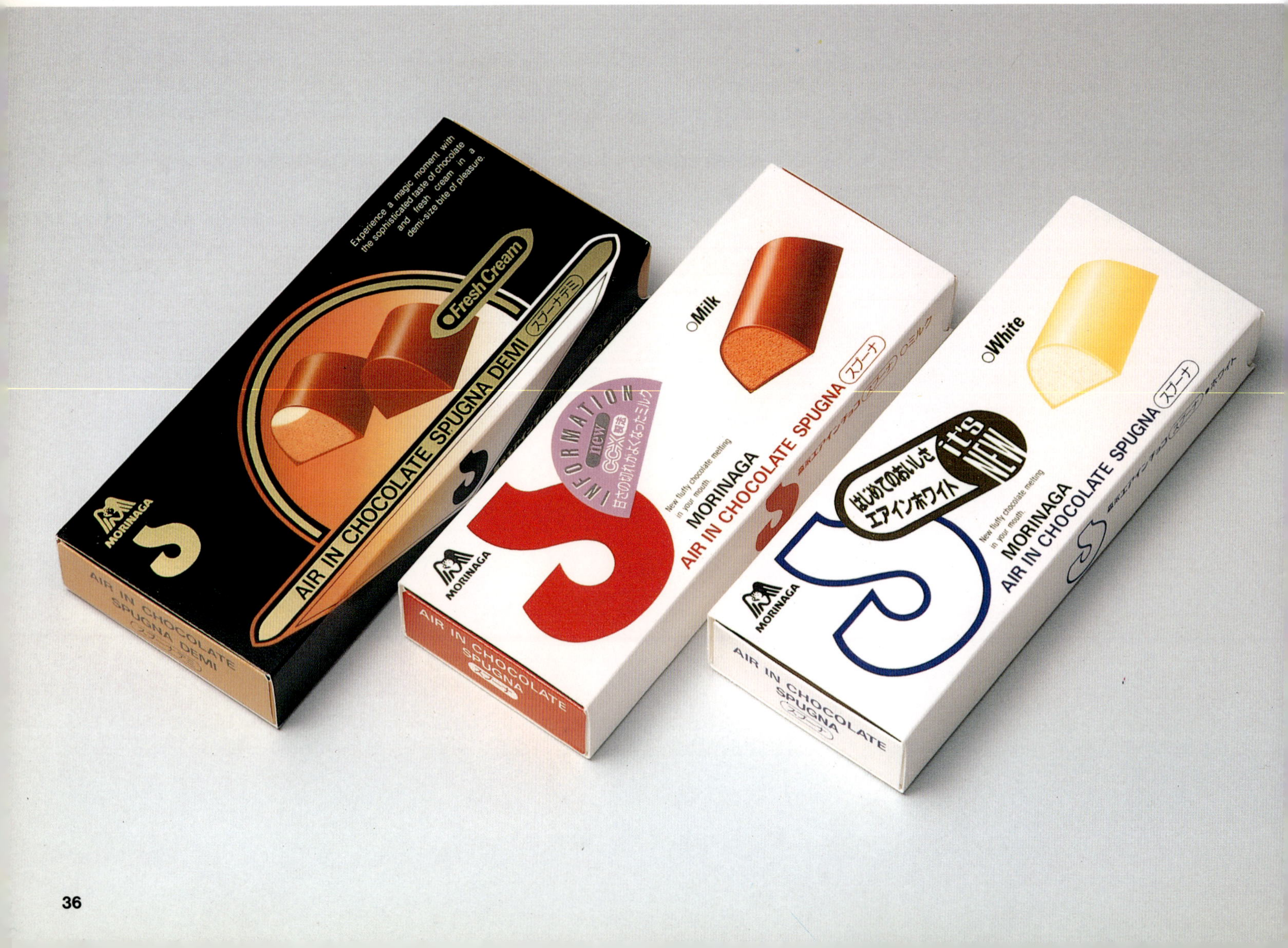

**28**
焼酎
AD—橋本近雄・麻布デザイン
LD—新保欣也・真藤 哲
PD—新保欣也
A—博報堂
C—宝酒造
1990

本書に収録された作品のなかで一番新しい商品がこの宝焼酎〈アレフ〉である。広く親しまれている焼酎“純”シリーズの新製品だが，ついにヘブライ語が登場することになった。
アルファベットの祖先であるヘブライ語の第1番目の文字，Aにあたるのがalephであり，これは後にギリシャへ渡って，alphaとなるのだが，純アレフは，“第一番”“最高峰”という意味をこめて名付けられた。シンボルはその第一番目の文字をデザインしたものである。

**28**
Shochu(Liquor)
AD—Chikao Hashimoto, Azabu Design
LD—Kinya Shinbo, Akira Shindo
PD—Kinya Shinbo
A—Hakuhodo Inc.
C—Takara Shuzo Co., Ltd.
1990

The newest product among those in this book is Takara Shochu's “aleph”. This is a new product of the well-known shochu 'jun' series, introducing at long last Hebrew into the marketplace. 'Aleph', the first letter of the Hebrew alphabet, ancestor of the modern English alphabet, is 'A' in English. This later became 'alpha' in Greek, but in the jun' series, it signifies the top, the highest. The symbol is the design of the first letter.

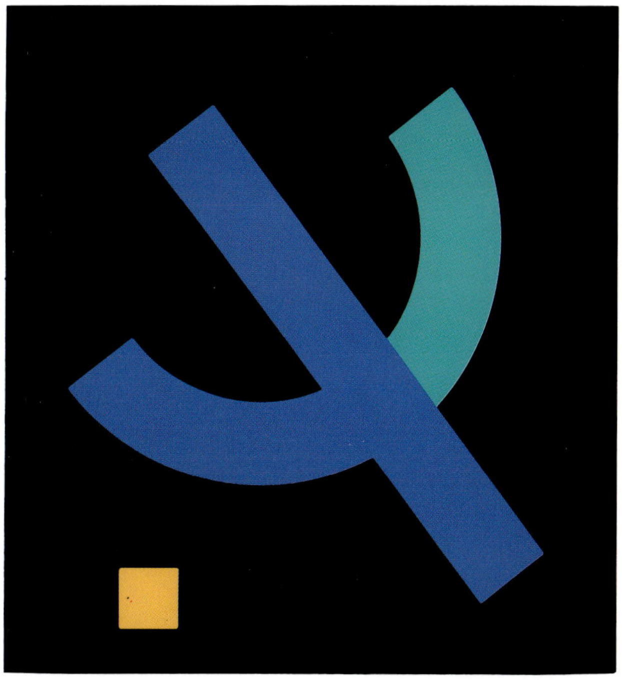

**29**
ポテトチップ
AD—塩沢大一
D—ワールドデザインセンター
C—エスビー食品
1990

数字もまた有用なモチーフだ。1とか100がくり返し使われるのは理解できるが，では，このエスビーのポテトチップはなぜ5/8か。それまでの同社のチップはひと口で食べるには大きすぎたので，食べ易い大きさを検討して，もとの5/8のサイズにしたという訳である。
意表を突いた分数によるネーミング，それを斜線を生かして巧みに構成したダイナミックなロゴタイプが効果的である。90年に入ってから三原色の斜線が加えられ，一段と華やかで力強くなった。

**29**
Potato Chips
AD—Daiichi Shiozawa
D—World Design Center
C—S & B Shokuhin Co., Ltd.
1990

Numbers are an effective motif. One can easily understand the well-used 1 or 100, but what is one to make of 5/8 for the SB potato chip? Previously, this company's potato chips were too big to eat in one bite, so they shrunk them down to 5/8 the size. Since no one ever thought that a name would be attached to a fraction, this successful and dynamic logo is especially effective, making good use of the oblique line of fractions.Since the start of 1990, a three-color oblique line has been added presenting a strong impression.

**30**
化粧品(スキンケア)
AD—片田博史
D—松山博之
C—ポーラ化成工業
1989

こんどは元素記号の登場である。酸素を与えて細胞を活性化し，お肌を美しくしようという女性用基礎化粧品シリーズ。$O_2$は言うまでもなく酸素分子のことであり，それをストライプ入りにアレンジして装飾性を備えることに成功した。写真でおわかりのように金箔押し加工である。古代朱とでも言うような容器の色も独特で美しい。

**30**
Cosmetics (for skincare)
AD—Hirofumi Katada
D—Hiroyuki Matsuyama
C—POLA Chemical Industries Inc.
1989

And now we come to the introduction of a chemical element's symbol into the market. This foundation cosmetic series for women activates cells by providing them with oxygen. Needless to say, O2 is an oxygen molecule. This is arranged in stripes and succeeds well in its decorative expression. As can be seen from the photo, this is goldleaf pressed. The dark reddish color of the container is unique.

**31**
レギュラーコーヒー
AD—デザイン室341・池田幸哉
LD—駿東 宏
PD—浜中将幸
A—博報堂
C—キーコーヒー
1990

新潮社の新情報誌〈03 TOKYO Calling〉とタイアップして売り出した2種類の缶入りレギュラーコーヒーである。03はもちろん東京の市外局番。ロゴタイプも雑誌のそれと共通したものを使い，30歳前後のコーヒー党都会人に焦点を合わせた商品であり，当然，誌上で広告展開がなされる訳だ。コクがあって香り豊かなBR，浅煎りで軽いタイプのLS，いずれもフーツラボールド体が実にセンスよく生かされている。

**31**
Canned Coffee
AD—Design room 341, Koya Ikeda
LD—Hiroshi Suntoh
PD—Masayuki Hamanaka
A—Hakuhodo Inc.
C—Key Coffee Inc.
1990

These are 2 types of canned regular coffee sold in conjunction with Shinchosha's new information magazine "03 'TOKYO Calling". 03 is, of course, Tokyo's city code. The logo and the magazine's 03 are used in combination to focus on city-dwelling coffee freaks around 30 years of age. It's quite natural to advertising development in magazines. BR is rich and aromatic, LS is a light type of coffee. Futsura bold lettering is taken advantage of in both cases.

**32**
男性用整髪料
CD—山下正和
AD—金子陽一
LD, PD—中井一郎
C—資生堂
1987

渋谷を東西によぎる国道246号線は，青山通りを中心に，いつも若者のあふれているルートである。そこからヒントを得て名付けられたのが資生堂の男性用洗髪，整髪料〈246〉で，これは単なる偶数の等差数列ではないのだ。その辺が分かるとこのデザインの面白さは倍加する。数字だけによる大胆にして繊細な，清潔感あふれるロゴタイプだ。

**32**
Hair Care Products
CD—Masakazu Yamashita
AD—Yoichi Kaneko
LD,PD—Ichiro Nakai
C—Shiseido Co., Ltd.
1987

Route 246 running east-west in Shibuya is always packed with young people, especially around Aoyama Street. Taking a hint here, Shiseido has named its shampoo and hair care products for men "246". Once you understand that this is not just an even arithmetic series, the design becomes more interesting, a dynamic yet delicete logo full of a sense of cleanliness.

**33**
アイスクリーム
CD—江崎グリコ広告部
LD, PD—パッケージング・クリエイト
C—江崎グリコ
1986

常時17種類の味を用意しているので〈17 seventeen ice〉と呼ぶ自動販売機用のアイスクリームである。
それぞれのパッケージには，味の頭文字が切り文字風のイラストとして入っており，これがひとつひとつ，みな可愛らしく，楽しさと同時に多品種を識別する記号の役目も果たしている。ここでは，蓋の部分に共通して使われているロゴマーク“17”を代表として掲載した。

**33**
Ice Cream
CD—Ezaki Glico Co., Ltd. Advertising Department
LD,PD—Packaging Create Inc.
C—Ezaki Glico Co., Ltd.
1986

This is a vending machine ice cream called “seventeen ice” and which is always available in 17 types. In each package, the flavor's first letter is placed in the illustration as cut letters to represent cuteness and fun and at the same time serving as a symbol for distinguishing a variety of types. Further, the logo mark 17 is written on the tops.

**34**
食品(フレーク，フロースト)
AD—田中康夫
LD, PD—永島 学
C—シスコ
1989

---

商品名に起用される数字の中では，100が圧倒的に頻度が高い。大半が，何らかの意味で100%を説明するのに使われるが，このシスコの〈CISCORN 100〉はズバリ¥100。1回分くらいのフレーク，フローストが少し薄型のパッケージに入った手頃な値段のシリーズであり，それを，フレークの形状を連想させる100の切り文字で分り易く表現している。

**34**
Food (Flakes)
AD—Yasuo Tanaka
LD,PD—Manabu Nagashima
C—Cisco Co., Ltd.
1989

---

Among numbers which promote product names, 100 is by far the most used to explain, for one reason or another, 100%. However, the 100 of "CISCORN 100" means 100 yen. Flakes in a somewhat thin package for one meal is a reasonably-priced series. The flake-like shape of the 100 is to make the fact that the product costs 100 yen easy to understand.

CISCORN
100

**35**
ジュース
CD—梅田悦史
AD—松田安司・宮地睦明
D—入沢滋彦・細沢充子
C—味の素
1988

私たちはもう，人工着色，人工甘味のジュースを食卓でとることはほとんどなくなった。果汁100%でなくてはジュースじゃない——100という数字は無条件に安心させる力をもっている。
これが典型的な100%ジュースのデザインだ。よく熟したオレンジの切口を背景にしたオープンフェイスのロゴタイプ。スクリプト体のオレンジの花も添えられた親しみ易いデザインである。

**35**
Juice
CD—Etsufumi Umeda
AD—Yasuji Matsuda, Nobuaki Miyaji
D—Shigehiko Irisawa, Mitsuko Hosozawa
C—Ajinomoto Co., Inc.
1983

We hardly drink artificially colored or flavored juice at the dinner table anymore. If it's not 100%, it's not fruit juice. This 100 has the power to assure us unconditionally. This is a typical 100% juice design with a well-ripened slice of orange in the background and an open face logo. Script lettering and an orange leaf are arranged to present an intimate design.

**36**
食品（牛乳）
D—藤重日生
A—アドジャパン
C—チチヤス乳業
1985

食品の製造年月日を容器に記すのは義務づけられて常識化しているが，その日付印を郵便スタンプの形を借りて積極的にロゴタイプとしてデザインにとり込んだユニークな試みのパッケージである。日付のところだけ黒の別刷りになっているのが，いかにも真実味があって頼もしい。また，自社経営の牧場からの直送品ということで，無駄を省いて簡素にまとめた外装の清潔感も好ましい。

**36**
Milk
D—Teruo Fujishige
A—AD Japan
C—Chichiyasu Nyugyo Co., Ltd.
1985

Here the logo is nothing more than the date of manufacture in the form of a postal stamp, creating a most unique design. Only the date is black and therefore seems realistic. The package is simple and clean, sent direct from the pasture, adding to the uniqueness of the design.

**37**
栄養剤
AD—吉岡博恭
D—吉岡博恭・武田薬品工業ヘルスケア事業部
A—宣弘社
C—武田薬品工業
1989

ビタミン剤というと，従来は横線も太くしたカタカナのロゴタイプが多かったが，それも年とともに様変り。この武田薬品工業の〈HICEE-L〉のスマートさは，明らかにストレスや不健康に悩む都会人，若々しい肌を持ち続けたい女性をターゲットにしたデザインだといえる。ビタミン＝レモンイエローという日本人の平均的な色彩感覚に基づいた黄色1色のパッケージも明るくて健康的だ。

**37**
Nutrients
AD—Hiroyasu Yoshioka
D—Hiroyasu Yoshioka, Takeda Chemical Industries, Ltd. Healthcare Division
A—Senkosha Advertising Co., Ltd.
C—Takeda Chemical Industries, Ltd.
1989

The smartness of this "HICEE-L" design from Takeda Chemical Industries, Ltd. is aimed at city dwellers with their complaints of stress and poor health and young ladies hoping to retain youthful skin. The single-colored package in yellow represents the brightness of health based on the Japanese perception of color that vitamin C = lemon yellow.

**38**
化粧品
CD—杉浦俊作
LD—ヘルムート・シュミット
PD—広 哲夫
C—イプサ
1987

〈IPSA〉はスキンケア，ヘアケアなどの基礎化粧品のブランド名であり，同時に社名ロゴマークでもある。
周囲に何もなければ，ロゴタイプはどんなに小さくても十分コミュニケートできる——と主張しているような洗練されたデザインだ。IPSAはラテン語でyourselfの意味。Iがなぜ折れているのか。いや折れているのではなく「Iを重複し強調して，I am I, つまり自らの美を創る」とシュミット氏は説明してくれた。

**38**
Cosmetics
CD—Shunsaku Sugiura
LD—Helmut Schmid
PD—Tetsuo Hiro
C—Ipsa Co., Ltd.
1987

IPSA is both the foundation cosmetic brand name for skin and hair care products and the company logo. With nothing in the perimeter, no matter how small the logo is, sufficient communication of the product has occurred. This is a polished design, almost insistent. IPSA means 'yourself' in Latin. But why is the 'I' bent? Well, it's not—it is stressed, saying, "I am I," creating beauty of self, explains Helmut Schmid.

**39**
男性用化粧品
AD—田辺弘基
LD, PD—野崎靖紀
C—ライオン
1985

時代の空気というか，よく似た作品が現われることがしばしばあるものだ。しかしライオンの〈f-in〉は明らかにiの点が折れて傾いている。初めて見たときは，おっ，と思わず首をiと同じ方向へ傾けて眺め，以後ながく記憶に残っている——そんな不思議な力をもっているデザインと言えないだろうか。
洗顔，先髪，整髪など各種そろったシリーズ商品で，帯の色によって内容を区別している。

**39**
Cosmetics for Men
AD—Hiroki Tanabe
LD, PD—Yasutoshi Nozaki
C—Lion Co., Ltd.
1985

The 'i' of Lion's "f-in" is clearly slanted. When I first saw this, I bent my head in the same direction as the 'i' without thinking. Since then, I have never forgotten this product with its seemingly mysterious power. The content of each product varies according to the color of the belt around the container such as facial soap, shampoo, hair care products, etc.

**40**
薬用化粧品
CD—熊井保亥
AD—池田修一
LD—ヘルムート・シュミット
PD—池田修一
C—資生堂
1985

UVとはUltra Violetつまり紫外線のこと。有害な紫外線から肌を守り，手入れをするための乳液，クリームなどの薬用化粧品が〈UV WHITE〉である。
白とパールの地色に，光沢銀の箔押しによる細身のUVロゴタイプ——これ以上ないと思われる繊細極まりないデザインだ。パッケージ上部が帯状に黒くなっているのは，実は鏡面仕上げの銀箔押しの部分である。

**40**
Medicated Cosmetics
CD—Yasui Kumai
AD—Shuichi Ikeda
LD—Helmut Schmid
PD—Shuichi Ikeda
C—Shiseido Co., Ltd.
1985

UV means ultra violet. UV WHITE is the name for medicated cosmetics such as milky lotions or creams which protect the skin against harmful UV rays. With white and pearl as background colors, the U and V are thin, silvery, foil-pressed letters, making for a rare delicate design. The black upper portion of the package is a mirror surface finish.

**41**
レギュラーコーヒー
AD―マキシム アート プラン，
片山恵子
LD, PD―上田優子
C―日本珈包印刷
1988

MerveillE＝驚嘆すべきもの，つまり素晴らしい味のコーヒーという意味であろうか。珍しく缶に直接印刷しないで，紙に印刷したものを巻いてある。手漉き和紙に似た暖かい手ざわりの紙だ。
細長いサンセリフ体に渋い色の影をつけた洒落た味わいのロゴタイプ。花の模様が入ったあたりは少し紅茶のイメージだが――。

**41**
Coffee
AD―Maxim Art Plan, Keiko Katayama
LD, PD―Yuko Ueda
C―Nihonkouhou Printing Co., Ltd.
1988

MerveillE＝something surprising. Perhaps the delicious taste of coffee is the intended meaning. The design is not printed directly onto the can as is usually done, but onto paper which is then pasted onto the can. The paper is soft to the touch, resembling handmade Japanese paper. This is a fashionable logo in thin, long letters sans serif with quiet colored shadows. The portion with the flower print evokes an image of tea.

CAFÉ
MerveillE
カフェ・メルヴェイユ

HALFTIME
TRADE MARK

**42**
飲料
CD—垣内貞夫
AD—和田 亨
LD, PD—阿部 優
C—日本たばこ
1988

日本たばこは，たばこ以外の事業もいろいろ行なっているが，自動販売機を中心とした一連の飲料のブランドが，このHALF TIMEである。時計の文字盤を思わせるこのブランドマークは，どこかとぼけたユーモアがあって楽しい。
当初はこのマークの位置が全て同じレイアウトで統一されていた（ORANGE ADEが当時のままのデザインである）が，シリーズが充実するにつれて，コーヒーのようなデザインのものが発売されるようになった。

**42**
Drink
CD—Sadao Kakiuchi
AD—Toru Wada
LD, PD—Masaru Abe
C—Japan Tobacco Inc.
1988

Japan Tobacco manufactures a variety of products besides tobacco. HALFTIME is one of its vending machine-centered drink series. This brand mark which evokes a watch dial contains a bit of blank humor making it somewhat amusing. In the beginning the mark's position were all the same (like ORANGE ADE). Later, however, to satisfy the needs of the series, a coffee-like design was put out.

**43**
チョコレート
AD—中川憲造
D—延山博保・森上 暁
A—旭通信社
C—明治製菓
1988

明治のマーブルチョコレートといえば長い間，円筒形の小さなパッケージに入っていて，子供たちが持っていたのをよく見かけたものだが，それがご覧のような袋入りに変身した。
中身の一粒一粒のイメージを大粒な同心円で象徴し，どの袋を開けても全ての色のチョコが出てくるような色彩計画がなされている。ロゴタイプは読み易く，覚え易い正統派である。

**43**
Chocolate
AD—Kenzo Nakagawa
D—Hiroyasu Nobuyama, Satoshi Morikami
A—Asatsu
C—Meiji Seika Co., Ltd.
1988

Meiji's Marble Chocolate had for the longest time been packaged in a cylindrical container often seen in the hands of children. As you can see, however, the package has been transformed into a bag. The image of the contents — single drops of chocolate — is represented by a single large circle. All color chocolate covered colors can be found in all packages. This orthodox logo is easy to read and remember.

**44**
医薬品
AD—水野卓史
D—宍戸 隆
C—久光製薬
1985

筋肉の疲労や痛みにシュッとひと吹き。爽やかなレモンの香りが漂って，すぐに痛みが引いていくような，気持ちのよいツインカラーのエアーサロンパス〈RAARA〉。
普通に組んだら長くなって隙間ばかりになる文字を，全部重ねて字間を詰めて，読む前に見るだけで理解できるような，簡潔なロゴタイプに仕上がった。

**44**
Medical Products
AD—Takushi Mizuno
D—Takashi Shishido
C—Hisamitsu Pharmaceutical Co., Inc.
1985

"RAARA" is a comfortable, twin-colored, aromatic lemon air salonpas for relief of pain due to sore, tired muscles. If the letters RAARA are written out in a usual print style, too much space would exist between each letter. By connecting all the letters and eliminating the intervals, the impression given is that you may understand what the product is even before reading. Thus this logo is quite concise.

**45**
肌粧品
D—木村 勝
C—ヒノキ新薬
1986

肌粧品，つまり肌を守る基礎化粧品のことだが，肌の状態は一定のサイクルで変化するものらしく，それに合わせて30種類もの肌粧品が用意されているという。檜の葉のシルエットの具体性と，オプチマ・メディウム＋直線エレメントの冷たい抽象性とが見事に調和して，シャープな切れ味のロゴタイプ，そしてタイポグラフィのデザインとなった。肌の奥まで透けて見えるような透明度の高いデザインと言ってよいと思う。

**45**
Cosmetics
D—Katsu Kimura
C—Medical Cosmetics Hinoki
Shinyaku Co., Ltd.
1986

This is foundation cosmetic skin care products for skin protection. The condition of the skin changes in consistent cycles. Accordingly, here are 30 types of skin care products. The concreteness of the cedar leaf silhouette harmonizes well with the cold abstraction of the optima medium plus straight lines. That presents a sharp logo which became a typographical design, a purportedly extremely clear design.

HINOKI
CLINICAL

**46**
ダイエット食品
D―ホーネンコーポレーション
C―ホーネンコーポレーション
1988

ダイエット食品もいろいろなタイプの商品が出ているが，ロゴタイプの面白さではこれが1番。午前7時の朝食を，カロリー減らしてさっぱりすませようという訳で，〈a nice AM.7:00 DIET〉と名付けられた。カップの中身はブレッド3枚と，コンソメスープの素＋はちみつが入っているもの（写真左）と，コーンスープ＋ブルーベリージャムのもの（同右）の2種。どちらも時計の文字盤に，クローバーやとうもろこしのワンポイントイラストで午前7時を表現した。説明しすぎるほどの商品名を実にセンス良くまとめている。

**46**
Diet Food
D—Honen Corporation
C—Honen Corporation
1988

There are numerous diet food logos, but this is the most interesting. The name "A nice AM 7:00 DIET" was created to encourage a low-calorie light breakfast. Both have a one-point illustration-clover or corn in the watch dial to express 7:00 am. the product's name is sufficient explanation, yet the design is well organized.

**47**
紅茶
AD—中村直行
D—浜 英男
P—山本弘之
A—パドラムクリエイティブ
C—日本紅茶
1988

文字通りティーポットのシルエットを中心にした〈TEA POT CLUB〉。おなじみのBROOKE BOND TEAのティーバッグである。
扇形とV字形でバランスをとり，黒を生かした芯の強いデザインだ。外箱にモノクローム写真を使ったところも粋で，落ち着いた印象を与える。

**47**
Tea Bags
AD—Naoyuki Nakamura
D—Hideo Hama
P—Hiroyuki Yamamoto
A—Padrum Creative
C—Brooke Bond Tea
1988

The logo "TEA POT CLUB" focuses on a silhouette of a teapot with well-known BROOK BOND tea bags. Balancing the V with the upper portion of a pie shape, this is a strong design making good use of black. The coolness of the monochrome photo gives a settled, relaxed impression.

**48**
ヘアケア
AD—奥村昭夫
D—野上周一
A—三幸社
C—牛乳石鹼共進社
1989

牛乳石鹼のヘアケア〈ONE　DAY〉は，everydayの意味だと筆者は解釈している。毎日，それも朝，洗髪するのが流行しているが，ONE DAYで今日も，明日も爽やかに，というわけである。
色の数字1の上に黒でONE DAYとのせていた第一世代から，製品がリニューアルされて少し手直しされた，淡い中間色の色帯が，その数字の1のイメージを引き継いでいる。

**48**
Hair Care Products
AD—Akio Okumura
D—Shuichi Nogami
A—Sankosha
C—Cow Brand Soap Kyoshinsha
1989

This writer understands that "ONE DAY" hair care means everyday hair care. It is popular to shampoo every morning. Previously, ONE DAY was written on a colored '1'; this has been renewed a bit in its second generation with the image of a '1' against pale colors.

**49**
キャンデー
CD—菊地伸介・柳沢光二
D—駒形克己
A—電通
C—大沢商会
1987

からだはミニなのに，大きい顔をして威張っているのが，このミントキャンデー〈BY ZERO〉である。普通のガムなどと同じサイズのパッケージだから，収まりきらずに二面にわたってレイアウトされることになった。ひとつを90度回転させて並べると，やっと人の顔をしたBY ZEROのロゴタイプが現われる仕組みになっている。小さいサイズでも迫力があるから，大きな図版で見ても決して大味にならない骨格の強さがある。

**49**
Candy
CD—Shinsuke Kikuchi, Koji Yanagisawa
D—Katsumi Komagata
A—Dentsu Inc.
C—J Osawa & Co., Ltd.
1987

The mint candy, “BY ZERO” presents a brazen, puffed up image, in spite of its smallness. It is the same size as regular gum, but as if all of it could not be put into the package, the lay out divides it into two parts. With the 2 parts together, a human-like face results. Although small, the impact is strong.

SAPPORO

BREWED FOR YOUR UNIQUE ENJOYMENT FROM FINE MALT, CEREAL GRAIN, SELECT HOPS AND PURE WATER WITH SAPPORO'S SUPERIOR CERAMIC FILTRATION TECHNOLOGY.

サッポロ 生 ビール

非熱処理

DRAFT BEER

**50**
ビール
AD—勝岡重夫
D—勝岡重夫・平出敏雄
C—サッポロビール
1989

字数の多い単語を横一列に組んで，ドラフトビール〈SAPPORO〉は，細くならずくどくならず，Aに洒落気も残して，スマートなロゴタイプになった。細い囲み線も黒一色の文字群の印象を柔らかくするのに効果的だ。2種類の金を使ったラベルがリッチであり，金星なんて，サッポロビールはどうしてこんないいキャラクターを持っているんだ，と思ってしまう。

**50**
Beer
AD—Shigeo Katsuoka
D—Shigeo Katsuoka, Toshio Hiraide
C—Sapporo Breweries Ltd.
1989

With characters laid out horizontally, they are neither too thin nor too much, and the missing horizontal line of the A adds fashionability to this SAPPORO draft beer logo. The thin black line surrounding the group of black letters gives a soft but effective impression. The two shades of gold adds richness, and with one gold star above the lettering, one wonders why SAPPORO has such nice characters.

**51**
清涼飲料
CD—明治製菓
AD—星野健三
LD—藤本 泰
PD—星野健三・藤本 泰
C—明治製菓
1988

カリフォルニアの風とともにやってきたアメリカンタイプの果汁入り飲料——頭にUSとあることによって，それと分かるのだが，できる限り原産国のムードを表現しようと努力した跡がよく理解できるデザインだ。星や果実のイラストのタッチが乾いた感触を与えるのも，そのためだろう。

**51**
Soft Drink
CD—Meiji Seika Co., Ltd.
AD—Kenzo Hoshino
LD—Yasushi Fujimoto
PD—Kenzo Hoshino, Yasushi Fujimoto
C—Meiji Seika Co., Ltd.
1988

The American type drink containing fruit juice arrived with a Californian breeze.With US written at the top of the cans, one could notice they were from the US. This design, however, intimately expresses American feeling. The sense of dryness in stars and fruit perhaps come from this.

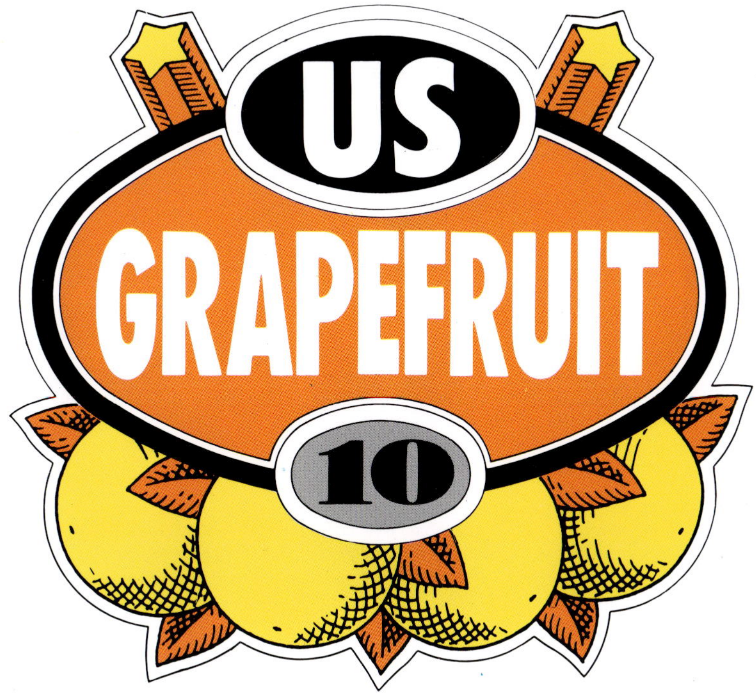

# Gaines

**52**
ペットフード
AD—松永 真
D—松永 真・鳩貝浩司
I—ピーター・ワーナー, ピーター・ケトル
A—東急エージェンシー
C—味の素ゼネラルフーヅ
1988

ロゴタイプだけを見る限りは，そう変化のない極太のフーツラボールド体（Gだけはユニバース風）なのに，パッケージに仕立てられると，俄然，光彩を放って生き生きとしてくる，そんなロゴタイプだ。縦にレイアウトして動感を，黒1色にして力感を，そしてもう一項つけ加えるなら，すてきな犬と猫の絵が，この商品の魅力を増幅している。

**52**
Pet Food
AD—Shin Matsunaga
D—Shin Matsunaga, Koji Hatogai
I—Peter Warner, Peter Kettle
A—Tokyu Agency Inc.
C—Ajinomoto General Foods Inc.
1988

Just looking at the logo, there is no novelty. Although it's only Futura Bold (only the G is like Universe), once written on the package, it suddenly shines. By writing vertically, it expresses movement. Black alone expresses vigor. A picture of a dog and cat would increase the charm of this product.

**53**
洗口液
CD―田辺弘喜
AD―富樫泉吉
LD―渡辺孝一
PD―富樫泉吉
C―ライオン
1988

口の洗浄液にふさわしい，いかにも爽やかな製品本体の色彩が，まず目につく。斜体にしてスピード感をもったユニバース系のロゴタイプから延びる2本の色の帯が，清々しい空気の流れを表わしていて気持がよい。そして，全ての要素を同系色の濃淡でまとめた手腕も手慣れたものだ。

**53**
Mouth Washing Liquid
CD—Hiroki Tanabe
AD—Senkichi Togashi
LD—Koichi Watanabe
PD—Senkichi Togashi
C—Lion Co., Ltd.
1988

First of all, the refreshing colors matching the mouth washing liquid of the products themselves catches one's attention. Two color lines stretching the from slanted Universe type logo with a sense of speed expresses the relieved flow of air. It represents comfort. Expressing all elements with lightness and darkness of the same kind of color is quite skillful.

**54**
レギュラーコーヒー
D—ホイ・リン・チュウ
C—キーコーヒー
1989

この作品はそもそもキーコーヒーのシンボルマークである。文字の部分を1行に続けて組んだサブマークや，鍵の部分を除いたワンセンテンス・ロゴマークなども含めた，CIシステムの中心となるものだ。それは同時にブランドマークでもあり(写真右)，またブルーのスクエアを缶全体に拡大して使う(同左)などして柔軟に適用している。
ブルーとイエローの色の対比も鮮やかで，長い間，親しまれて使われていくだろうと思う。ディテールを言えば，鍵とKとの境界の造形処理も実に巧みだ。

**54**
Coffee
D—Hoi Lin Chu
C—KEY Coffee Inc.
1989

In the first place, this work is the KEY coffee's symbol mark. It's the center of the C.I. system including the submark-letters continuously arranged into one line, and the one-sentence logo excluding the drawing of the key. At the same time, this is the brand mark (right picture). Further, the blue square is enlarged on the whole can and used (left picture). I believe that the bright contrast of yellow and blue will be used for a long time. The process of designing the border between the key and the K is especially skillful.

**55**
ストアブランド
CD—田中良弘
D—川路ヨウセイ
C—ジャスコ
1986

ジャスコの自社ブランド〈WHITE BRND〉は，消費頻度の高い日常型の商品を，一切の無駄を省いて低価格で提供することをめざして設定された。
包装は簡素，デザインも赤1色のブランドロゴにキャッチフレーズを添えるだけで，それ以外のデザインは何もしないというシンプルな手法。その代り，全品を極力，一ヵ所で群として販売する方法がとられる。実質本位の姿勢を "WHITE" ととらえたわけだ。

**55**
Store Brand Name
CD—Yoshihiro Tanaka
D—Yousei Kawagi
C—Jusco Co., Ltd.
1986

Jusco's 'WHITE BRAND' was established to provide a frequently consumed everyday product free from all waste. The wrapping is simple. The design with a single red logo and catch phrase is also simple. Instead, as much as possible, all products are sold at one place as a group. The primary substance is regarded as 'WHITE'.

WHITE
BRAND
ムダを省いて、くらしをサポート

Kefran
TaKaRa
Mone
BOSTON CLUB
SUNTORY WHISKY
Coca-Cola
Sprite
Oligo CC
Cooking Wine Suntory
POKKA
Welch's
AQUARIUS
SIMBA DARJEELING TEA
Vege Take
KIRIN 午後の紅茶
Choya
ROKKO WATER
sinvino
Fe++
UCC WORKS AFTER WORK
KIRIN 烏龍茶
Misty Valley
Fanta
アセロラ C200
Jazz'In
Sulco
KYOWA
C1000
鉄骨飲料
NIKKA WHISKY
サントリー ウーロン茶
アサヒビールの麦茶
QUICK & WELL
CANADA DRY
Asahi PF21

LOTTE
CHEWING GUM
89.12.27製造
ENERGY
CHARGE BIT
チャージビット パワーチャージキャンディ
オリゴプラス飴
グレープフルーツ味
はちみつレモンC
Vitamin100mg
SUPER FLAVONO
LOTTE CHEWING GUM
EXCELLENT TASTE AND FLAVOR
鉄骨飴
SUPER BLACK BLACK
LOTTE CHEWING GUM
EXCELLENT TASTE AND FLAVOR
ピュアプルーン
FUJIYA CANDY
フルーツファイバー入り
Fruity
PEACH
Fruity
GREEN APPLE
ひとつぶにリンゴ10個分のビタミンC
シェントアプフェル
ひとつぶにレモン4個分のビタミンC
LIMON
シェントリモン
9粒入 100円
ひとつぶにレモン4個分のビタミンC
ACEROLA
シェントアセロラ
C-100α
Glico gum
KissMint
気分さわやかリフレッシュ用ガム
50円(税別)
Glico gum
KissMint
香りエレガンス お口の香り用ガム
Glico gum
KissMint
さわやか森林浴 リラックス用ガム
Glico gum
KissMint
お口が香る、エチケット用ガム
ヨーグリーナ
ogurina
ヨーグルトキャンディー
つぶつぶ果汁
ストロベリー
SOFT CANDY
ヨーグルト
ソフトキャンディ
EROLA
OTTE CANDY
QUICKWIT'S
Espresso
IMPRESSIVE TASTES GUARANTEED TO BRIGHTEN YOUR DAY
QUICKWIT'S
Blueberry Mint
QUICKWIT'S
Chili Mint
QUICKWIT'S
Alaska Mint
QUICKWIT'S
レモンミント
QUICKWIT'S
Black Mint
タブレット
HARIS GUM
コーヒー
眠気スッキリ
タブレット
HARIS GUM
ハーブ
リラックス
CALPIS
オリゴCC キャンディ
Oligo CC
新素材[ビフィズス活性キャンディ]
MORINAGA
hi CREAM
white
hi CREAM
milk
Asahi プロテイン キャンディ
PF21 アサヒ ピーエフ21
GREEN ROSE
お口のエチケットキャンディ
OA CANDY
HICHEW
MORINAGA
SOFT CANDY
BY ZERO
FREE ZONE
歯につかないガム
義歯にもつかないニュータイプガム
SUPER SUPPAI GUM
GRAPE FRUIT
スッパさ120%
RUM ENA SCOTCH
BUTTER ENA SCOTCH
MINT ENA SCOTCH
MORINAGA
眠れない珈琲
キャンデー
アセロラキャンディ
COFFEE 259
MENTHOL CANDY
SHE HER HER
Super Emission
SUPERIOR MINT
シーハーハー
SHE HER HER
CITRUS LEMON
SHE HER HER
VALENCIA ORANGE
SHE HER HER
WINDS
LIGHT CALORI
WINDS
SUGARLESS GUM
ティカロ
Cmint
1枚わずか 1kcal
SUGARLESS GUM
ミント・シー
mint C
SUGARLESS GUM
LOTTE
Blue Berry
LOTTE
COFFEE
LOTTE
ACEROLA
LOTTE
CHEWING GUM
VAPOR ACTION
HALLS
ホールズ
2in1 WITH RETSYN
チュピ
Chupi
vitamin C candy
ハレンシアオレンジ
GUM
MINT

**56**
日焼け止め化粧品
CD—杉浦俊作
AD—松原正毅
LD—川崎修司
PD—金子 節
C—資生堂
1986

Intercept vt. ①途中で押える，進行をさえぎる ②遮断する——つまり，肌に有害な紫外線をカットするための乳液やファンデーションだ。
長方形の中にヘルベチカ体を組んだだけなのに，頭文字Iを斜めに差し込むというわずかなテクニックが，たちまち鋭敏な感覚のロゴタイプを出現させる。

**56**
Cosmetics for Preventing Sunburn
CD—Shunsaku Sugiura
AD—Masaki Matsubara
LD—Shuji Kawasaki
PD—Takashi Kaneko
C—Shiseido Co., Ltd.
1986

Intercept vt. 1) to arrest in progress, interrupt the progress, 2) to shut down, i.e., a foundation or lotion for shutting out harmful UV rays. Even though the lettering is simple Helvetica within a rectangle, the technique of slanting the 'I' suddenly makes the logo very sharp.

**57**
女性用リップクリーム，コロン
AD—花王
LD—アトリエ・ディナン
PD—花王
C—ニベア花王
1989，1990

図版は拡大してお見せするが，本来は小さなサイズで使われるロゴタイプである。女性用のリップクリームやコロン，デオドラント（体臭防止剤）のためのものだから，商品本体に使われる大きさは40ミリ足らず。両サイドの小さな正方形がつぎつぎと色変りして，楽しく，可愛らしいデザインだ。掌中で愛でるといった趣がある。

**57**
Lip Cream, Cologne
AD—Kao Corporation
LD—Ateliers Dinand
PD—Kao Corporation
C—Nivea Kao Co., Ltd.
1989, 1990

Here, originally small logos have been enlarged. The actual size of the logos for the lip cream, cologne, and deodorant for women is less than 40 mm. The 2 small squares at each side of the lettering differ according to product variations.

58
レギュラーコーヒー
CD—川島 保
D—藤掛正邦
A—電通
C—上島珈琲
1989

半年ほど前に，JAL（日航）のAの字の横線がないことの是非が新聞の投書欄で論じられたが，デザインの現場では，誰が使い始めたということなく横線のないAは是認されている。上向きの三角形はみなAなのである。このAromageも大胆に変形したAを頭に据えることで，印象を決定づけた。焙煎のグレードを示す楕円のシールが，豊かな香り（aroma）を保証しているように美しく輝いている。

58
Coffee
CD—Tamotsu Kawashima
D—Masakuni Fujikake
A—Dentsu Inc.
C—Ueshima Coffee Co., Ltd.
1989

Approximately a half year ago, the appropriateness of JAL's missing horizontal line of the 'A' was discussed in the readers' column of a newspaper. In the field of design however, it was approved without discussions of propriety, for everyone reads an 'A' if the apex of the triangle is pointed upward. Similarly, A in 'Aromage' is easily understood and determines the impression. The oval sticker indicating the grade of roasting and brewing shines brilliantly as if it were ensuring a rich aroma.

**59**
コーヒー用クリーミング
AD—岩井 一
D—窪田仁志
C—ネッスル
1988

ネッスルの〈Brite〉は，コーヒー用のクリームのパッケージとしては，ほぼ完全にデザイン上の要件を備えていると思う。内容にマッチした白くて清潔なキャップとラベル，柔らかいがしかし力強くて明快なロゴタイプ，その，珈琲色ではなく，といって金赤のように浮き立たない落ちついたえんじ色の色彩，パウダーとリキッドの別を示すワンポイント写真など，発売当初から，筆者はずっと，ストアの陳列棚に讃辞を送ってきた。

**59**
Coffee Cream
AD—Hajime Iwai
D—Hiroshi Kubota
C—Nestlé Co., Ltd.
1988

Nestlé's 'Brite' contains, I believe, all the essential elements of a coffee cream package design. The clean white cap and label matching the contents are soft, yet represents a strong and lively logo. Not the color of coffee, but a somewhat settle reddish-gold, the product is separated into powder and liquid varieties.

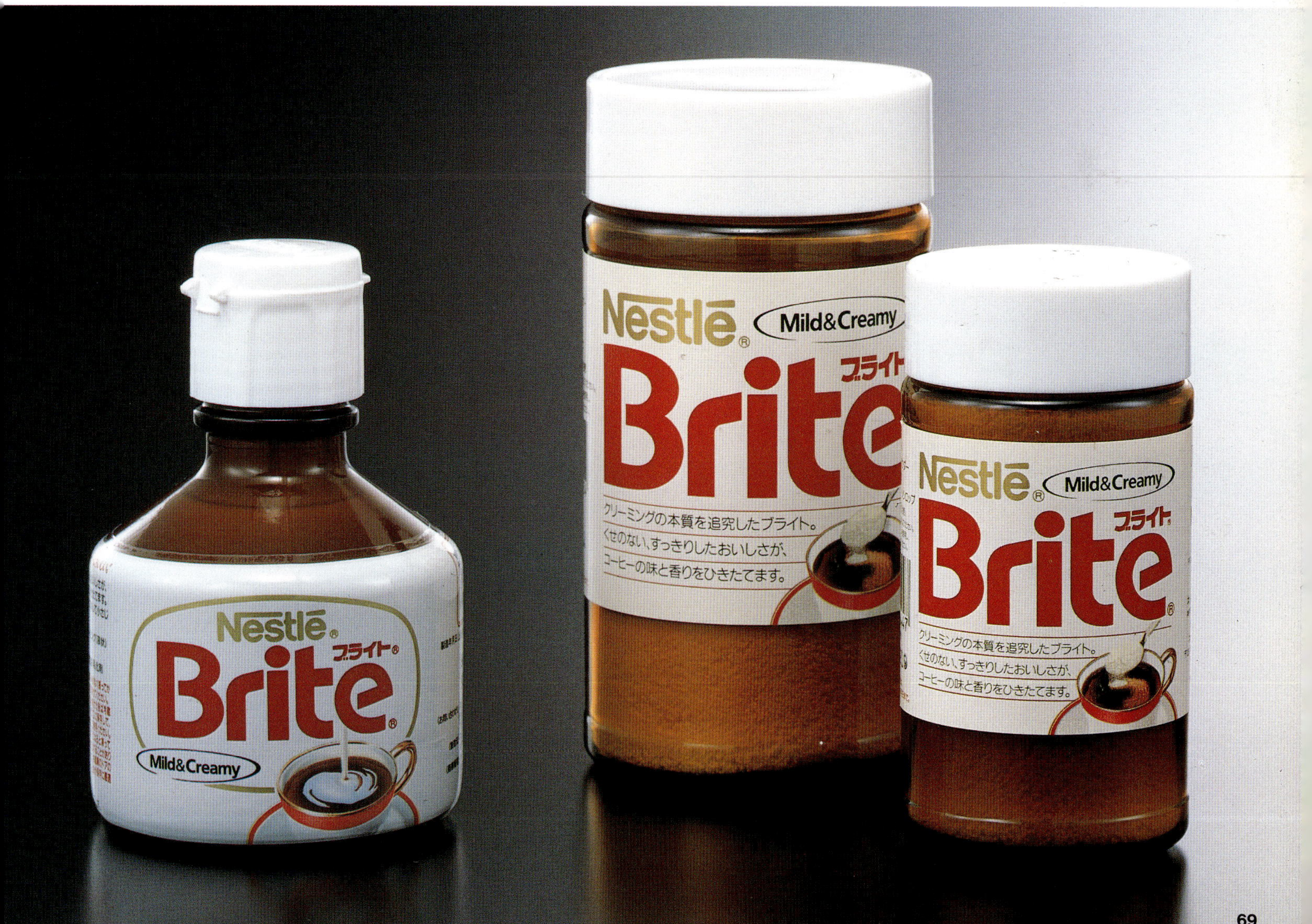

そのつど新鮮
エアカット方式

# café in bottle

**60**
濃縮コーヒー
CD—福寿 誠
AD—八幡功一
D—高橋哲久
A—博報堂
C—ホーネンコーポレーション
1989

これは驚きのコーヒーである。ボトルを軽く振ってからノズルをカップに向けて2〜3秒押すと，ムース状のコーヒーが出てくる。これに湯を注げば出来上りという便利なものだ。そのことをイラスト入りでデザインしたのが〈café in bottle〉のロゴタイプである。初めての試みだから図解が必要であったし，これがアイキャッチャーとして親しまれることになったのは幸せであった。

**60**
Coffee
CD—Makoto Fukuju
AD—Kohichi Yawata
D—Akihisa Takahashi
A—Hakuhodo Inc.
C—Honen Corporation
1989

Shake the bottle and squeeze the coffee mousse into a cup for about 2 or 3 seconds. Add hot water and voila! Thus the logo, 'café in bottle.' Since this was a first attempt, an instructive photo was necessary.

**61**
食物繊維飲料
LD, PD—ヘルムート・シュミット
A—エヌ・アイ・エイ
C—大塚製薬
1988

発売した年に3億本（！）を売り上げて，機能性飲料のトップを走るのが，〈FIBE MINI〉である。
飲料の色によくマッチした淡いピンク・オレンジのラベルと，2行に区切った，無機的にも見える黒いロゴタイプとが奇妙につり合って，不思議なムードを発散している。米誌「ニューズウィーク」がcute little bottleと呼んだのも同じ印象を述べたものだと思う。

**61**
Nutrient Drink
LD, PD—Helmut Schmid
A—NIA
C—Otsuka Pharmaceutical Co., Ltd.
1988

Its first year out, 'FIBE-MINI' sold 300 million bottles and was tops in the nutrient drinks class. The light pinkish-orange label matching the color of the contents and the inorganic black logo are strangely balance, evoking a somewhat mysterious mood. Newsweek had the same impression, calling this one a "cute little bottle."

FIBE-
-MINI

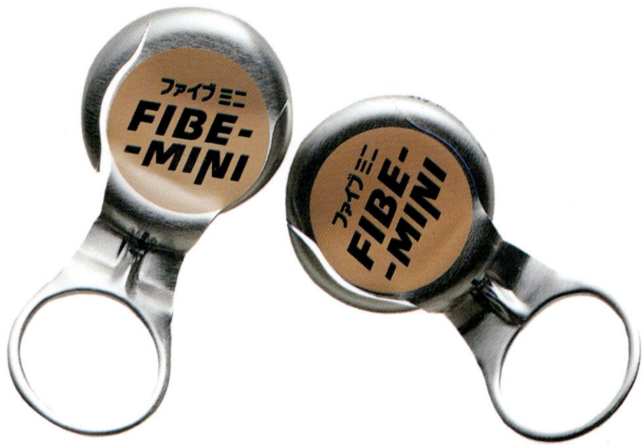

**62**
洋生菓子(シュークリーム)
D—カンパニー・スタイル
C—洋菓子のヒロタ
1989

洋菓子のヒロタも'89年にCIを導入した。パッケージの右上に小さく見えるTHE HIROTAの文字が，CIシステムの中核となるロゴマークであり，そのOを形作るドットパターンをデザインキャラクターとして，商品の包装へ展開されることになった。
洋菓子のヒロタといえば，まずシュークリームだ。先のドットパターンを共通項として5種類の味ごとに文字と色を変えた，ソフトでチャーミングなロゴタイプが使われる。他にシューアイスのパッケージも一新された。

**62**
Confectionary
D—Company Style, Inc.
C—The Hirota Confectionery, Inc.
1989

HIROTA , an occidental confectionery, introduced C.I. in 1989. THE HIROTA, seen in small print at the upper right of the package, is the kernel of the C.I. system's logo. The design of the dot-pattern O became an integral part of the packaging. HIROTA is famous for its cream puff. The logo type is soft and charming, with each of 5 products using different colors but sharing the dot pattern. The ice-cream puff package has also been renewed.

**63**
アイスクリーム
CD—明治乳業
AD—本州製紙パッケージングセンター
LD, PD—藤村 敬
C—明治乳業
1988

なんといってもアイスクリームは季節物だし，専用の冷凍ボックスに入れて売られているから，買った人でないと目に付きにくいのが残念だ。この明治〈F･Y･G〉も筆者は直接店頭で目にしたわけではないことをお断りしておく。F･Y･Gはフローズンヨーグルトの略か。端正でクールなタイポグラフィ，冷たい感触に徹した配色など，これは大人向けのアイスクリームだ。“甘すぎないから健康的だ” とも書かれているし——。

**63**
Ice Cream
CD—Meiji Milk Products Co., Ltd.
AD—Honshu Paper Co., Ltd. Packaging Center
D—Kei Fujimura
C—Meiji Milk Products Co., Ltd.
1988

Since ice cream is seasonable food, it is sold from special freezers. Therefore only people who buy ice cream would notice their designs. I did not actually notice Meiji's F·Y·G ice cream in shops. Is F·Y·G an acronym for frozen yogurt? The typography is clear cut and cool, and its coloring focuses on a sense of coldness, and adult-oriented ice cream.

**64**
モーターオイル
AD—福田繁雄
D—村 武史・鈴木良彦
A—電通
C—共同石油
1988

食品や化粧品ばかりでなく，産業用品にもこのような美しいパッケージを発見すると嬉しくなってしまう。
共石のモーターオイル〈21〉シリーズは，もちろん21世紀がテーマ。お分かりだろうか。色のスペースの左側に2の字のシルエット，そして黒いスペースで1を表わしている。謎解きのようなロゴタイプである。パターンとして見てもシンプルでスピード感に満ち，Very goodだ。

**64**
Motor Oil
AD—Eisuke Fukuda
D—Takeshi Mura, Yoshihiko Suzuki
A—Dentsu Inc.
C—Kyodo Oil Co., Ltd.
1988

It is a pleasure to find such a beautiful package not only in food or cosmetics but also in industrial products. The theme of Kyodo motor oil '21' series is the 21st century. On the left side of the color part, there is a 2 in silhouette. The black line expresses the number 1. This is a logo like a riddle. Even looking at it as a pattern, it offers a simplicity and fullness of speed.

**65**
化粧品
D—グラフィック・トラフィック
C—マックスファクター
1986

化粧品のパッケージは，ときに，うらやましいくらいに豪華で凝った作りのものを見かけることがあるが，その典型がこれ。マックスファクターのPAZZAZシリーズ。図版中央のグレーの三角形の部分が，実は鏡面仕上げになるべきところなのだ。パステルカラーのパターンの中に，手にとった女性の顔がキラッと写るという仕掛け。この場合，おろそかにされている訳ではないが，PAZZAZの文字は脇役になっていると見てもよいだろう。

**65**
Cosmetics
D—Graphic Traffic
C—Max Factor Co., Ltd.
1986

Sometimes, one enviously sees luxurious and elaborate cosmetic packages. Max Factor's PAZZAZ series is a typical example. The grey triangular part in the middle of the picture should actually be a mirror. The face of the woman who picks this up will be reflected in the pastel pattern. This is the gimmick. In this case, it can be said that 'PAZZAZ' takes a back seat to the gimmick.

C-LAND

*every child has its own land.*

**66**
ステーショナリー
D—三菱鉛筆
C—三菱鉛筆
1987

正しくは，これはブランドロゴタイプであって，パッケージのためだけに作られたものではない。
鉛筆，消ゴム，筆入れ，ノート，はさみ，のりなど，一連の学用品が全て，赤，青，黄，緑のブランドカラーの組合せでできている。そして，その中心となるワードメッセージが〈C.LAND〉である。
LEGOを連想しない訳にはいかないが，漫画やゲームの低俗の世界とは隔絶した，企業の良心を見るような商品づくり。鮮やかの一語に尽きる。

**66**
Stationery
D—Mitsubishi Pencil Co., Ltd. Japan
C—Mitsubishi Pencil Co., Ltd. Japan
1987

Truthfully, this is a brand logo, not made only for the package. A series of stationery items such as pencils, erasers, pencil cases, notebooks, scissors, and glue are produced in combination of brand colors such as red, blue, yellow, and green. The key word is 'C-LAND'.

**67**
チョコレート
D―佐藤勝則
C―森永製菓
1987

森永製菓の〈Hi-CROWN〉チョコレートも息のながい商品である。格調高く，高級感を売りものにしたパッケージの時期もあったが，'87年にデザインが現在のように変更された。
ロゴタイプだけを見ると直線的で硬く感じるが，十分な余白と甘くソフトな配色で，チョコレートのベストドレッサーとなった。ロゴの背後にあるパターンも，内容を表わす言葉の頭文字が素材となっていて，左からm.w.sである。

**67**
Chocolate
D—Katsunori Sato
C—Morinaga & Co., Ltd.
1987

Morinaga's 'Hi-CROWN' chocolate has been around a long time. Its package used to represent high class and dignity, but the design was changed to this present one in 1987. Looking only at the logo, it seems rather stern, yet it stands at the top of chocolate designs with its ample white space and soft coloring. The pattern behind the logo is the first letter of the word representing the contents, which are, from left to right, m, w, and s.

**68**
オーディオ・カセットテープ
CD—植村 徳
AD—高橋 敏
LD, PD—高橋 敏・籠 邦博
C—TDK
1987

シガレットケースというものがこんな形をしていたように記憶している。角を取って丸味をつけ，ポケットなどにするっと入りそうなカセットテープ。ヘッドホン用に作られたTDK〈IF〉シリーズは黒と白の2種類。とくに黒をベースにして黄色い楕円と共に鮮やかに浮かび上がる方のIFがNOWである。黒白の両方のスペースにまたがって文字がネガ・ポジに分かれるデザインが，この頃よく流行した。

**68**
Cassette Tape
CD—Noboru Uemura
AD—Ving Takahashi
LD, PD—Ving Takahashi, Kunihiro Tohshi
C—TDK Corporation
1987

This shape reminds us of a cigarette pack. Yet it is a cassette tape with rounded corners for ease of sliding into a pocket. The TDK series made for headphones comes in 2 colors—black and white. The design with a black base showing 1F in a yellow oval clearly stands out. The design in which 1F is divided into negative and positive was quite popular at the time.

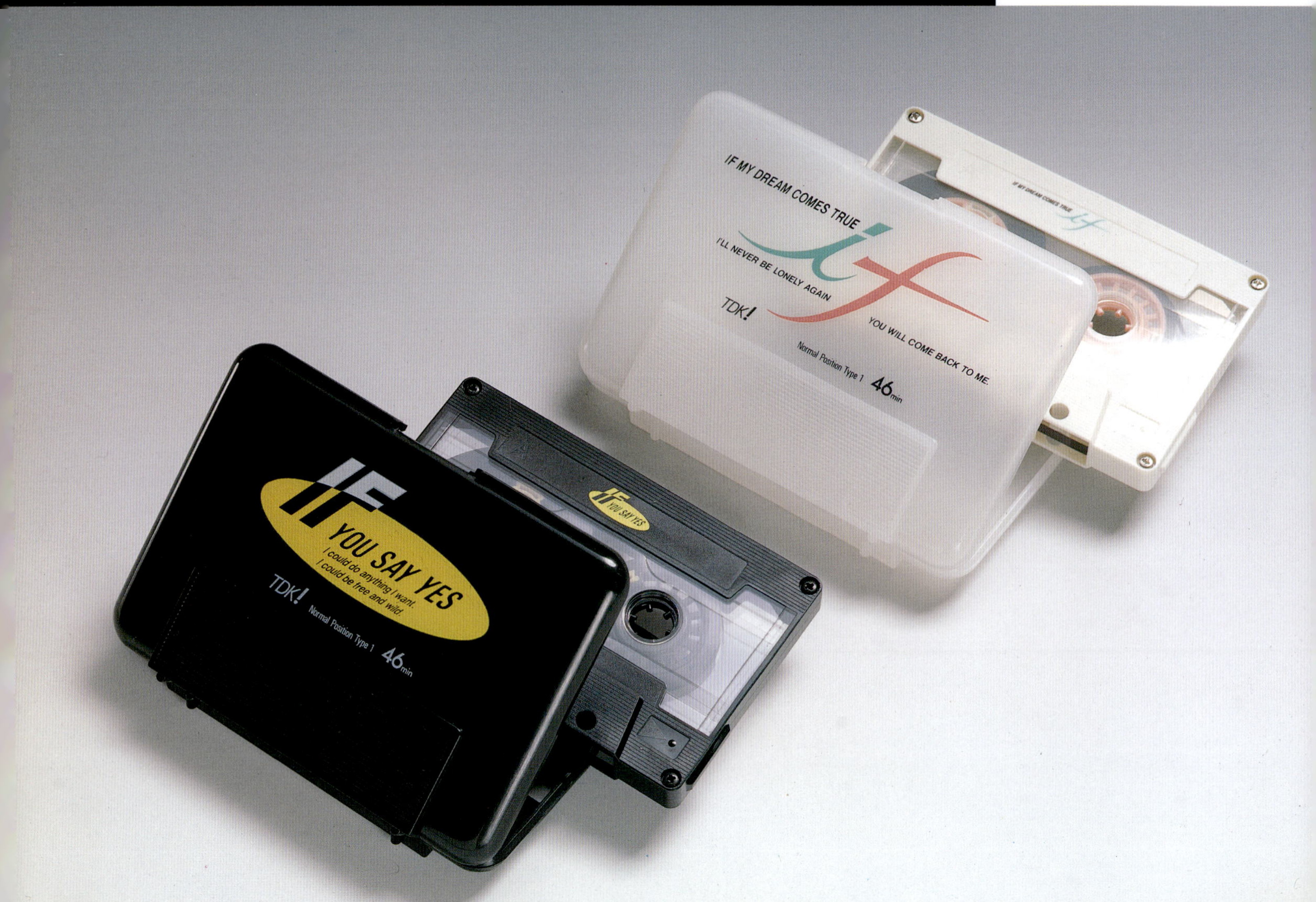

**69**
アイスクリーム
AD—村 武史
D—加藤貴穂・時政美枝
C—明治乳業
1988

Premium, Personal, Popular, Pioneer, Single, Select, Simple, Super——PとSのつくことばを集めてこの商品を特長づけたので〈PS(ピーズ)〉コレクションと言う。極力色彩を抑えてクールな表情を装った，アダルト向きのデザインだ。商品コンセプト，デザイン共にアダルトだが，アダルトがアイスモナカを食べるかどうかとなると，どうだろう。

**69**
Ice Cream
AD—Takeshi Mura
D—Mizuho Kato, Yoshie Tokimasa
C—Meiji Milk Products Co., Ltd.
1988

This product is called the 'PS' collection for it amasses numerous P and S sounds—Premium, Personal, Popular, Pioneer, Single, Select, Super. Presenting a cool image avoiding the use of color as much as possible, this is an adultish design. The product concept and design are adultish, and this is fine, but it is questionable whether or not adults will eat such an ice cream wafercake.

scottie

**70**
ティッシュペーパー
AD—松永 真
D—松永 真・鳩貝浩司
A—マッキャンエリクソン博報堂
C—山陽スコット
1986

生活空間に猥雑なものを持ち込まないこと，それがデザインの使命なのだ——と，〈scottie〉を見るたび，使うたびに諭されているような気がする。無印良品とは違う，十分に手を尽してシンプルに到達する。いつまでも市場に生き残ってほしいデザインの一つだ。
このロゴタイプは白抜きにして使ったときが，やはり一番美しい。

**70**
Tissue Paper
D—Shin Matsunaga
A—McCann-Erickson Hakuhodo Inc.
C—Sanyo Scott Co., Ltd.
1986

Whenever I see or use 'scottie,' I feel as if I am being taught that the mission of the design is not to bring squalor into life. This is not a simple generic brand, but one whose simplicity is the intentional result of enormous effort. This logo is most beautiful with white letters on a colored background.

**71**
ヘアケア
D—新里一裕
C—スワロー化研工業
1986

縦長の容器に横組みのロゴタイプを入れるのは，いろいろ工夫が要るものだ。〈COSMOREA〉の場合，幸運にも下方に開放されたMが単語の中央に来ている。しめた！と作者が膝を打ったかどうか。スワロー化研の方も，「おっ，いいじゃないか」とすぐにOKを出したであろうことは，十分想像できる。

**71**
Hair Care
D—Kazuhiro Shinzato
C—Swallow International Cosmetics
1986

Skill is required to horizontally arrange a logo on a rectangular container. The released M of COSMOREA fortunately falls in the middle of the word. One can easily imagine the creator slapping his knee and Swallow saying, "Oh! This is just fine" when this one was created.

KOIWAI

*It is a Healthy Refreshment Made*

YOGURT

*of Selected Koiwai Milk. KOIWAI*

DRINK

*YOGURT DRINK Relieves Your Thirst.*

小岩井ヨーグルトドリンク

**72**
ヨーグルトドリンク
D—PAOS
C—小岩井乳業
1988

小岩井乳業の乳飲料，清涼飲料には，共通して太丸ゴシック体によるKOIWAIの文字が使われていて，イメージの統一がなされている。この〈YOGURT DRINK〉も同じファミリーの書体で構成された，文字ばかりによるデザインだ。それにもかかわらず，楽しさがあふれているのは甘いソフトな色彩はもちろんだが，文字の字間を空けて容器全体に散りばめた，程よい装飾性によるものだ。

**72**
Yogurt Drink
D—PAOS
C—Koiwai Dairy Products Co., Ltd.
1988

KOIWAI uses log gothic lettering in their lactic drinks and soft drinks to attain a unified image. This is a YOGURT DRINK design whose letters come from the same family. The design is nevertheless full of a sense of fun, with sweet, soft colors and decorative phrases filling the ample space between letters.

**73**
インスタントコーヒー
AD—松永 真
D—松永 真・川上元美
A—博報堂
C—味の素ゼネラルフーヅ
1986

アウトラインをフリーハンドで仕上げた超特太コンデンス体を巧みに使いこなした〈Blendy〉。瓶の正面から商品名が一覧できて，しかも細った印象を与えないバランスが絶妙と言えよう。この商品のために用意したと思われる茶色のパールインキを使ったラベルも，渋い光沢を放って，インスタントコーヒーとは思えないような高級感がある。

**73**
Flavored Instant Coffee
AD—Shin Matsunaga
D—Shin Matsunaga, Motomi Kawakami
A—Hakuhodo Inc.
C—Ajinomoto General Foods Inc.
1986

'Blendy' is a logo whose outline was finished by hand and which skillfully uses super large block-condensed lettering. Indeed, this lettering was created especially for 'Blendy' and could doubtfully be used for any other product. Looking at the bottle from the front, the product name is readily apparent.

# Blendy

ROHTO

Zi

EYE PREPARATION

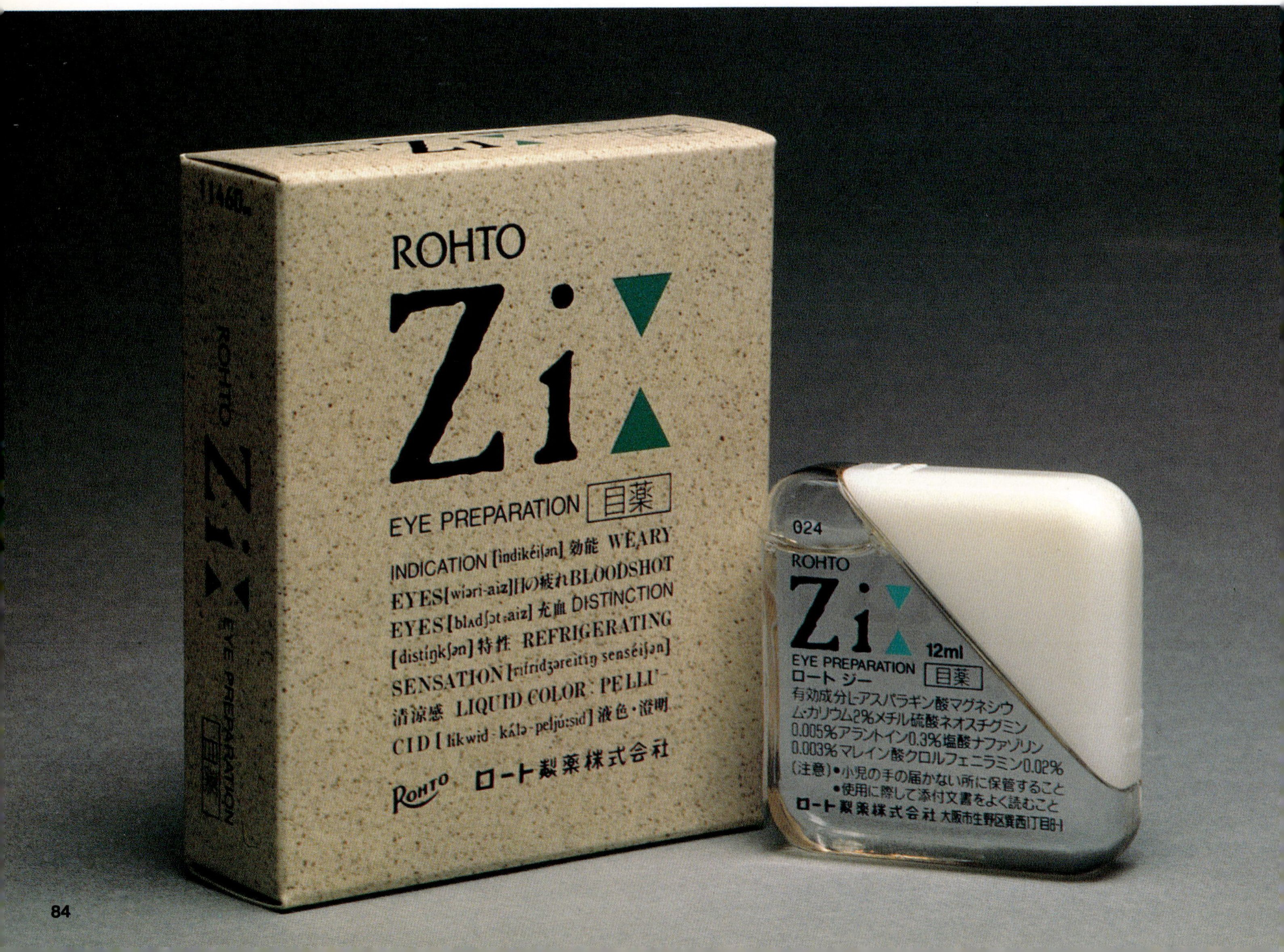


**74**
目薬
AD—Y工房
D—饒平名克郎
C—ロート製薬
1987

ロート製薬の目薬〈Zi:〉は，あくまでも発音記号にこだわる。ロゴタイプのみならず，効能書きまで発音記号入りで説明している念の入れ方。一種のアクセサリー的表現とみてさしつかえないだろう。ガラスの容器が不思議な フォルムをしていて，蓋を開けてみたい衝動にかられる。

**74**
Eye Lotion
AD—Y Kobo
D—Katsuro Yohena
C—Rohto Pharmaceutical Co., Ltd.
1987

ROHTO is particular about the phonetic image of its eye preparation, 'Zi:.' They are equally particular about their detailed explanation of the product. Its glass container evokes us to open it.

**75**
基礎化粧品
CD—岡田一朗
AD—宮城壮太郎
D—宮城壮太郎・有沢真太郎
C—ライオン
1988

自然で健康な素肌を保ちつづけるための洗顔料やローション，クリーム——こんな一連の基礎化粧品を表現するのに，ライオン〈upty〉は，手漉き和紙を模した紙張りのケース，フリーハンドによるヒューマンなタッチを残したままのロゴタイプを選定した。あるいは実際には，小さな印刷文字を拡大したのかもしれないが，それはともかく，しっとりと，静謐感の漂うデザインが完成した。

**75**
Cosmetics
CD—Ichiro Okada
AD—Sotaro Miyagi
D—Sotaro Miyagi, Shintaro Arisawa
C—Lion Corporation
1988

Lion's 'upty' selected a logo in which the human touch remains in freehand, and a case whose paper finish resembles Japanese handmade paper to express a series of basic cosmetics such as facial soap, lotion, and cream for natural healthy skin. In fact, however, they could have enlarged the small print. In any case, the design which represents the image of moist and tranquil is complete.

·upty·

**76**
洗顔フォーム
CD—岡田一朗
AD—内貴真弓
D—スタジオ・マック，河鍋春恵
C—ライオン
1989

ライオンの洗顔フォーム〈P'1(ページワン)〉はすでに二代目である。初めのデザインもワンポイントマーク風で愛着があったが，こうして技巧的な新しい顔に出会ってみると，前のP'1は少し幼なかったかなあという感想をもつ。ぬいぐるみの肌ざわり，しかも大きな動物のそれのような，たっぷりとした存在感がある。

**76**
Facial Foam
CD—Ichiro Okada
AD—Mayumi Naiki
D—Harue Kawanabe
C—Lion Corporation
1989

Lion's facial foam 'P'1 (page 1) is already the second design. The first design also had the one point mark image; however, upon encountering the artificial new design, the previous design seems a bit childish. With a texture like that of a stuffed animal, the design makes its presence felt.

**77**
パイ菓子
AD—ベーシックプロダクト
D—本多英二
C—信用社
1988

香ばしい醬油の味と洋菓子パイのドッキング，つまり和洋混交の新菓子ということで，和風の紙目に英文ロゴタイプを毛筆で書き上げた。泥くさ さと土産品とは思えないセンスとが同居している。
言い遅れたが，これは瀬戸大橋の真ん中，与島のリゾート基地・京阪フィッシャーマンズワーフのオリジナル特産品だ。ここは中国，四国の土産品が一堂に集まるところとして賑わっている。

**77**
Pie
AD—Basic Product Inc.
D—Eiji Honda
C—Shinyosha Co., Ltd.
1988

You can taste both savory soy sauce and a Western-style pie. This is a new pastry which blends the Japanese and Western styles. The logo using English letters is printed on its package made of Japanese style paper evoking both simple and sophisticated feelings. This is an original gift item of Keihan Fisherman's Wharf located in Yo-shima, an island appearing driving the middle of the Seto bridge.

**78**
ビール
D—PAOS
C—キリンビール
1989

れっきとしたビールなのに，これはもうソフトドリンク感覚のデザインだ。事実，味もあっさりとしたものらしいが，メタリックグリーンの地肌といい，スクリプト体によるロゴタイプの伸びのびとした流動感といい，炭酸飲料と見違えてしまうような爽やかさ，軽やかさである。そういえば麒麟の姿もどこか隅の方へ隠れてしまったようだし――。ビールの新感覚派宣言である。

**78**
Beer
D—PAOS
C—Kirin Brewery Co., Ltd.
1989

Although beer, the design of its can offers the feeling of soft drinks, refreshing in appearance and taste. The metallic green of the background color and the logo in script gives the refreshing, light impression of a soft drink. One can hardly see their trade mark, Kirin (an animal from old Chinese legend) in this new generation of beer.

**79**
ジュース
D—PAOS
C—小岩井乳業
1989

全身シルバーメタリックの装いに包まれた重厚なパッケージである。1ℓ入りだからずしりと重い。白抜きのメーカー名，繊細なスクリプト体による原材料名，そして100%を表示する色の数字，多くの要素を巧みに重ね合わせたロゴタイプは気品があって好ましい。ほとんどの人が読まないと思うが，英文のコピーが美しくレイアウトされているとなんとなく有難みが感じられて，今やデザインに欠かせないエレメントである。しかしこのKOIWAI 100%ジュースは，声高に叫んではいないのに，その格調の高さゆえに120%くらいの高級感があって，陳列棚でも異彩を放っている。

**79**
Juice
D—PAOS
C—Koiwai Dairy Products Co., Ltd.
1989

The metallic silver color gives an impression of solidity. It is heavy, containing one liter of juice. The name of the manufacturer in white letter type, the name of the ingredients by a delicate script type, and the number 100 which means 100% pure fruit juice-all these logos are ingeniously arranged and elegant in appearance. Although many people do not actually read the copy writing in English, it helps to make it look better, an essential element now in the graphic design world. Koiwai 100% Juice stands out on display stands by its noble style package producing the feel of high quality.

**80**
ティーン向け化粧品
CD—杉浦俊作
AD—松原正毅
LD—四田千絵子・樋口真貴
PD—四田千絵子
C—資生堂
1988

〈Chipie〉とは自己主張する女の子という意味のネーミングだそうだが，そろそろ自分の個性を自分で作ってみたくなるハイティーンあたりがターゲットだろうか。それにしてはリボンなんか結んだりして，あどけなさを残した可愛いロゴタイプだ。

**80**
Cosmetics for Teenagers
CD—Shunsaku Sugiura
AD—Masaki Matsubara
LD—Chieko Yotsuda, Maki Higuchi
PD—Chieko Yotsuda
C—Shiseido Co., Ltd.
1988

The name “Chipie” includes the meaning of girls asserting themselves. The target of this item seems to be girls in their late teens who want to create a self-image by themselves.In light of this, the logo with its ribbon, looks too cute and rather innocent. The message, then, appears to be that although they try their best to keep up with adults, they are still too young.

**81**
男性用化粧品
AD—大浜良友
LD, PD—梅沢一徳
C—エイボンプロダクツ
1987

同じフリーハンド体のロゴタイプでも，Chipieとは対照的にこちらは〈騎士＝Cavalier〉。言うまでもなく男性用の化粧品である。ブラッシュ体で一気に書ききった潔さがストレートに伝ってくる。現代の騎士はシャワールームと鏡の前で作られる。

**81**
Cosmetics for Men
AD—Yoshitomo Ohama
LD, PD—Kazunori Umezawa
C—Avon Products Co., Ltd.
1987

Using the same kind of handwritten style logo, this Cavalier for men produces opposite feelings from Chipie. The logo in brush type conveys a bracing feeling as if writing it in one forceful breath. Cavalier today is used at shower rooms and in front of mirrors.

Cavalier

**82**
釣り糸
AD—西田まさを
LD—西田まさを・蓮本和子
PD—西田まさを・蓮本和子・鷲塚伸彦・浜崎弘昭・野田公基・栗山圭史
A—大広
C—東レ
1987

珍しい商品ジャンルのロゴタイプをご紹介しよう。釣り糸である。巻きぐせや撚りがつきにくく直線性がすぐれている，擦れ，結節，引張りにも強さを発揮する，そんな特性を，真ん中を貫く一本の直線で表現した。たくさんの説明をていねいにレイアウトしたパッケージも，品質への信頼が出ていて好ましい。

**82**
Fishing Line
AD—Masao Nishida
LD—Masao Nishida, Kazuko Hasumoto
PD—Masao Nishida, Kazuko Hasumoto, Nobuhiko Washizuka, Hiroaki Hamasaki, Koki Noda, Keiji Kuriyama
A—Daiko Advertising Inc.
C—Toray Industries, Inc.
1987

Here we introduce a logo for an uncommon product-fishing line. The logo represents characteristic strength. Straightening, pulling, and rubbing, resistance to curling and difficulty of knotting are represented by the line pervading the logo. Package explanations are pleasing and express trust in quality.

Solaroam
golden fluorescent line

**83**
チョコボール
AD—江崎グリコ広告部
LD, PD—駒 芳昭・島川順子
I—河又正男
C—江崎グリコ
1989

墨くろぐろと書き綴った太めのブラッシュ体によるグリコの〈Bisky Ball〉が，菓子売場に山と積んであったときは壮観であった。発売当初，目にした光景である。その後，陳列台に納まったが，Bisky Ballはそのロゴタイプの力強さで，依然，他を圧倒している。

**83**
Chocolate Ball
AD—Ezaki Glico Co., Ltd. Advertising Department
LD, PD—Yoshiaki Koma, Junko Shimakawa
I—Masao Kawamata
C—Ezaki Glico Co., Ltd.
1989

The display corner heaped with Glico's 'Bisky Balls' in the confectionery section looked magnificent. It had just gone on sale. Although they are on usual display stands now, they still overwhelm other products with their powerful logos.

**84**
チョコレート菓子
CD—中川良二
AD—吉野正道
LD, PD—マイケル・ピータース
A—電通
C—明治製菓
1988

明治製菓〈body〉は徹底的に語呂合せと連想ゲームの世界だ。中身はチョコバーである。バー→バーベル→ボディビル→ボディ→エブリボディ→ガブリボディ，つぎつぎとことばの連想がかけ巡る。ロゴタイプも，正にbodyがバーベルを持ち上げている，語呂合せならぬ絵合せの図となった。アルミの光沢がバーベルの質感とピタリ一致する。

**84**
Chocolate Bar
CD—Ryoji Nakagawa
AD—Masamichi Yoshino
LD, PD—Michael Peters
A—Dentsu Inc.
C—Meiji Seika Co., Ltd.
1988

Meiji's 'Body' is like a word in the game Password. This is actually a chocolate bar, but the name invokes words such as bar—barbell—body building—body—everybody. And the logo suggests that the word 'bar' lifts a barbell. The metallic texture of the package is appropriate to the feel of barbell.

**85**
日本酒
AD—松永 真
D—松永 真・小堀賢一
A—クリエイティブ・グルーヴィ
C—福光屋
1988

金沢の清酒〈福正宗〉が，革新的なラベルで味とデザインを一新した。従来の日本酒の前近代的なラベルデザインとなんと隔たっていることか。小文字のfとmが着想のきっかけにはなっているが——と作者は打ち明けてくれた。しかしその痕跡はすでにどこにもなく，吟味され，彫琢されて，福正宗のシンボルは日本の紋章の域にまで昇華した。そういえば，と源氏香図紋を思い出す人がいるかもしれない。

**85**
Sake
AD—Shin Matsunaga
D—Shin Matsunaga, Kenichi Kobori
A—Creative Groovy, Inc.
C—Fukumitsuya Sake Brewery Co., Ltd.
1988

Fukumasamune, sake made in Kanazawa, changed its taste and design with an innovative label. it's quite different from the old-fashioned designs of traditional labels. The designer said that the clue to the idea had come from thinking of 'f' and 'm'. But the complete logo is carefully selected, and is sublimated just like a Japanese family crest.

**86**
食品(カレー)
CD—江崎グリコ広告部
D—博報堂大阪支社
C—江崎グリコ
1986

黒1色で使うロゴタイプはたくさんあり，強さ，重さ，硬さ，渋さなどいろいろな場面で使い分けられるが，グリコのカレー〈LEE〉の場合は "辛さ" である。茶色の地色の中にあって，一層辛味が増してきたように思う。箱の半分以上をロゴタイプが占めていて，自信のほどがうかがえる。ちなみに辛さは4段階あって，×1は普通の味，×5は額に汗がにじんでくる，×10は水なしでは無理，×20はピリッと身体全体に辛さが駆けぬける——と説明されている。

**86**
Curry
CD—Ezaki Glico Co., Ltd. Advertising Department
D—Hakuhodo Inc.
C—Ezaki Glico Co., Ltd.
1986

There are numerous logos in black. They are used in different ways depend on what image—powerful, heavy, hard, quiet, etc. the client would like to express through the use of black. Glico's Lee expresses hotness. It looks increasingly hot with brown in the color of the background. The logo using up more than half the surface of the package shows confidence. There are 4 levels of hotness: X1—ordinary, X5—your forehead will sweat, X10—cannot be eaten without water, and X20—the hotness runs through your body.

**87**
スポーツ飲料
D—カンパニースタイル
C—ダイドードリンコ
1988

数ある飲み物のうち，スポーツドリンクは確実にその一角を占めるに至った。このダイドードリンコの〈SE〉も発売されてから数年を経ており，パッケージのデザインも二代目，商品の評価も定着した。太い横線ばかりで構成したSPORTS ENERGYの頭文字SEは，無機的にさえ見え，アルミの地肌を積極的に生かしたクールなデザインと相まって，強じんなエネルギーが期待できそうなロゴタイプである。

**87**
Sports Drink
D—Company Style Inc.
C—DyDo Drinco, Inc.
1988

In the varied world of soft drinks, sports drinks has come to occupy a steady position. The well-known DyDo Drinco's SE has been sold for several years, and is currently into its second generation package design. SE is an acronym for 'sports energy'. The logo is constructed only by strong horizontal lines. It looks mechanical, as if supplying a powerful energy with its cool design making use of the metallic texture.

**88**
レトルト食品(カレー)
D—ホワイト
C—ライオン
1988

ライオンで販売するMcCORMICKブランドのレトルトカレー〈cilico〉も黒を基調にし，赤と組合せて辛さを表現した。メキシコ風味のカレーだから赤いパッケージがよく似合う。
Cの中にOをとり込んで左右のバランスをとることに成功した。
こちらは辛度7の強辛と，辛度3の弱辛の2種がある。

**88**
Pouch-packed Curry
D—White
C—Lion Corporation
1988

Lion sells the pouch-packed curry "cilico" as one of their products under the McCormick brand. The logo is based on black and red, representing hotness. Red for it's Mexican-style curry suits the image. The logo with its symmetry in the insertion of the 'o' into the 'c' is quite successful. There are 2 kinds: 3—slightly hot and 7—very hot.

iichiko

**89**
焼酎
AD—河北秀也
D—明星秀隆・石井康治
C—三和酒類
1985

この焼酎を飲んだ人なら知っていたかもしれないが，筆者はこの〈iichiko〉ということばの意味が，気になりつつもずっと分からなかった。この機会に取材したのでご報告する。大分県の方言で，いい＝良，ち＝よ，こ＝これ。つまり「良いよこれは！」という意味である。
ひらがなでそのローカル色を残しつつも，主役の部分は思いきって直線処理の英文で今日風にデザインし普遍性を獲得した。

**89**
Shochu (Liquor)
AD—Hideya Kawakita
D—Hidetaka Myojo, Koji Ishii
C—Sanwa Shurui Co., Ltd.
1985

Someone who has drunk this shochu might know the meaning of the name, but I didn't know it in spite of having given it much thought. I did, however, figure it out. Iichico means "This is good." in Japan's Oita dialect: "ii" means "good", "chi" means "is", and "ko" means "this". The logo remains simple in the Japanese portion, and uses sharp English letters in the main part. This works effectively to get both a refined image and universality.

**90**
石鹼
AD—宇田 優
LD, PD—広谷龍児
C　牛乳石鹼共進社
1989

なによりもまず，色の爽やかさで魅せられる作品である。そのさわやかさが製品の品質感をよく表わしていて，香りがたち昇ってくるようだ。石鹼のひとつひとつの包装は，ホワイトパールの地に白線を敷きつめた，繊細，清潔なもの。全ての角を丸くとった手ざわりの柔らかいロゴタイプに親しみを感じる。

**90**
Soap
AD—Masaru Uda
LD, PD—Ryuji Hirotani
C—Cow Brand Soap Kyoshinsha Co., Ltd.
1989

First of all, the color attracts people, and brings you a feeling of the product as if you can feel the fragrance. Each soap is packed in pearl colored paper with white stripes, appearing clean and delicate. The logo with its rounded edges gives a soft and warm impression.

NEW TYPE

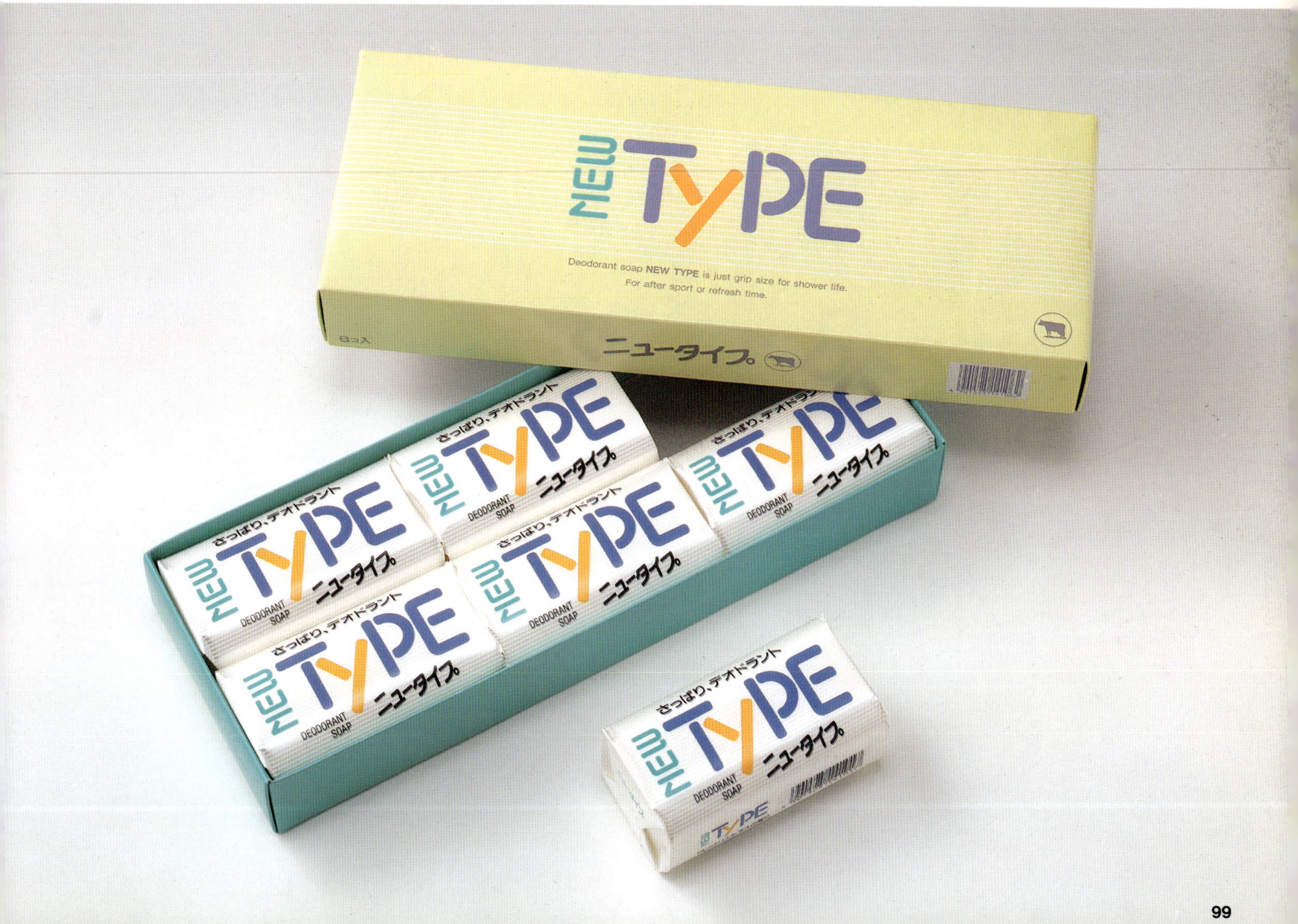

AGF
maxim®
ara-
bica
coffee

**91**
コーヒー
CD—田島 肇
AD—河北秀也
D—明星秀隆・谷井郁美
C—味の素ゼネラルフーヅ
1990

不思議な魅力をもったロゴタイプだ。まず1字1字のデザインが面白い。図版としては掲載してないが，ペアで発売したearl grey teaのgなど，ちょっと類を見ないユニークなフォルムだ。それを字間を空けてパラパラと組んだから，いよいよ不思議な，そして新鮮なロゴタイプになった。ボトルへのデザインも，巻き紙，貼り紙なしで，白1色刷り。実にシンプル&ストレートである。筆者も早速買って，眺めて，飲んでみたのだった。

**91**
Coffee
CD—Hajime Tajima
AD—Hideya Kawakita
D—Hidetaka Myojo, Ikumi Tanii
C—Ajinomoto General Foods Inc.
1990

This logo has a strange appeal. Each character is interestingly designed. Earl Gray Tea which is sold as its sister product also has an interesting logo, especially the 'g' in "gray" has an unprecedented unique form. As there is even more space between each character, it turns out to be more fresh and attractive in appearance. The design of the bottles with direct printing in white looks sophisticated.

**92**
コーヒー飲料
LD—平松 暁
PD—平松 暁・橋本博文
C—キャピタルフーズ
1990

Coffeeということばをロゴタイプにするとき，2字ずつ続くfとeをどう処理するかがデザインのポイントになる。続くことを幸に，なにもしなくても様になると考えるか，工夫をして続くことの面白さを発見するか。この場合は明らかに後者であろう。Cもfもeも，みな同じ方向性をもたせて，くり返しの面白さでまとめた苦心の跡が見てとれる。Oが少し邪魔だなあと感じたであろう作者には，デザイン上で同情の念が起こる。

**92**
Canned Coffee
LD—Satoru Hiramatsu
PD—Satoru Hiramatsu, Hirofumi Hashimoto
C—Capital Foods Co., Ltd.
1990

When you create a logo for coffee, the point of the design is to make 'ff' and 'ee' look neat. There are two ways. One is not to give it special form on purpose, the other is to make use of the interest in the doubled characters. For this coffee, the latter was chosen. One can see their intention to make all of the characters in the same rhythm to make the logo look smooth.

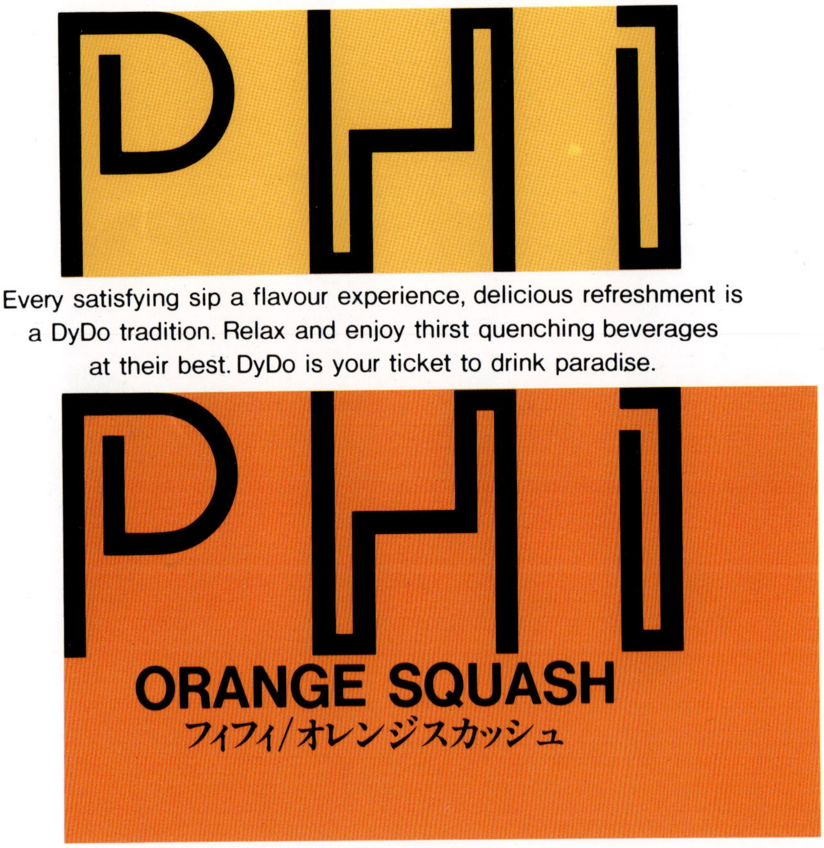


**93**
炭酸飲料
D—カンパニースタイル
C—ダイドードリンコ
1987

少し読みづらく，発音しにくいと思うが〈PHIPHI〉はフィフィと読む。一時期盛んに使われたワンラインの文字を使ってそれをくり返し，濃淡の同系色のバックと一体となって初めて完結するロゴタイプである。同じことばのくり返しは記憶され易く，5種類の仲間があって自動販売機の中にカラフルに並んでいると，どれにしようかと迷ってしまう楽しさがある。

**93**
Soda
D—Company Style, Inc.
C—DyDo Drinco, Inc.
1987

It must be difficult to read and pronounce the name, PHIPHI as it should be pronounced [fifi]. This type of lettering used to be popular. The logo uses one line for each character exactly as if writing without lifting pen from paper. And it's completed only on the two background colors of similar shades. Words with repeated syllables like PHIPHI are easily remembered.

**94**
化粧品
AD—木村 勝
LD, PD—木村 勝
PD—赤羽なつみ
I—高橋 枝
C—資生堂
1985

ティーンエイジャー向けの化粧品シリーズで，写真の他に，リップクリーム，乳液などがあり，種類毎に可愛いイラストが使われるが，〈ekubo〉のロゴタイプは全商品に共通して用いられる。
FAXで送信した文字を拡大するとこんな風になるのだが，その機械的な冷たい効果を，明るさと軽さへ見事に転化した，健康的で楽しいロゴタイプである。

**94**
Cosmetics
AD—Katsu Kimura
LD, PD—Katsu Kimura
PD—Natsumi Akabane
I—Eda Takahashi
C—Shiseido Co., Ltd.
1985

This is one of the series of cosmetics for teenagers. In addition to deodorant, they have lip balms, milky lotions, etc. Different, cute illustrations are provided for each product with the same logo applied through all the products in the series. They changed a cold, mechanical image of fax letters to a bright and light image creating a neat and happy logo.

YOU'LL FIND GOOD QUALITY IN OURS

Porcal

**95**
洋菓子
D—田中康夫
C—シスコ
1988

クラッカーの表面にいくつもの小さい穴があいている。それはサンドしたクリームをしっかり保持する効果があるのだと思うが，その凸凹した質感を文字のディテールで巧みに表現したロゴタイプである。正しくは，その質感にピッタリ合った書体を上手く選んだと言うべきだろう。しかし，既存の書体だからといってデザインの価値は不変である。

**95**
Confectionery
D—Yasuo Tanaka
C—Cisco Co., Ltd.
1988

There are many holes in the surface of crackers. They seem to exist to keep cream tightly between crackers. The logo here ingeniously represents the texture of crackers. Actually they chose the right letters, because they are the letters called 'Steve' in Instant Lettering.

**96**
コーヒー飲料
CD—第一企画
AD—星野健三
LD—星野健三・藤本 泰
PD—藤本 泰
A—第一企画
C—カネボウ食品
1988

テレビゲームの画面をそのまま持ってきたような，子供たちが喜びそうなデザインである。〈BOSE〉のロゴタイプはもちろんのこと，土星，流星，スペースシャトルなどのエレメントも全て細かい万線を用いて再現する。缶の周囲を宇宙空間が取り巻いて，正にミクロコスモスだ。うちの中学の坊主が，ファミコンに熱中しながら飲んでいた奴だな。

**96**
Flavored Instant Coffee
CD—Dai-ichi Kikaku Co., Ltd.
AD—Kenzo Hoshino
D—Kenzo Hoshino, Yasushi Fujimoto
A—Dai-ichi Kikaku Co., Ltd.
C—Kanebo
1988

This looks just like a TV game screen. Kids will like the package. Every element on the package including the logo is made with minute lines. The surface of the can looks like a microcosmos.

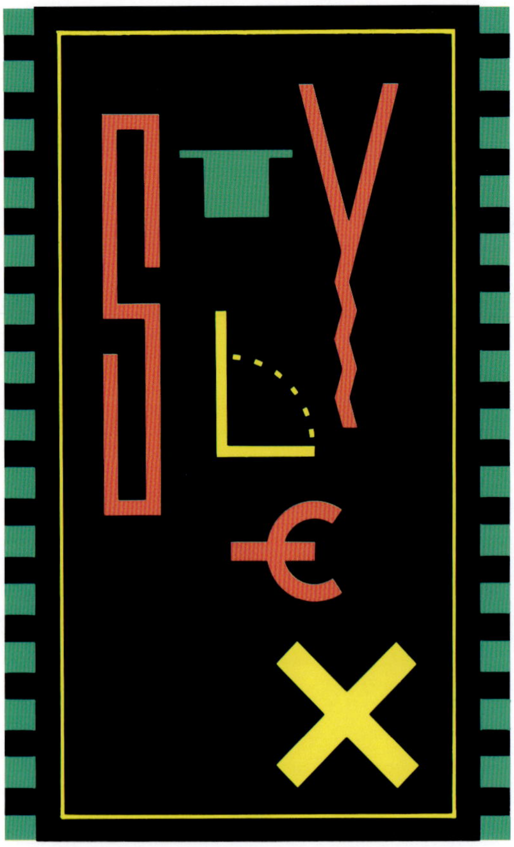


**97**
男性用整髪料
AD—森 幸男
D—久保雅彦
C—ポーラ化成工業
1989

読めますか？　この商品名。〈STYLEX〉です。ま，読めても読めなくても，高校生くらいの男の子は買っちゃいますよ。だって，メチャ面白いじゃん。文字はハチャメチャだし色もへんだけどさあ。これシール貼ってんだろ，な。びんもカッコいいじゃん。こんなのそこのコンビニに売ってたんだ，ラッキーだぜ！

**97**
Hair Care Products for Men
AD—Yukio Mori
D—Masahiko Kubo
C—Pola Chemical Industries Inc.
1989

Can you pronounce the name of this product? This is "Stylex". Whether you can pronounce it or not, high school kids will buy them because they look interesting. The letters are eccentric and the colors are strange. The labels are stuck on the packages and the bottles are cool.

**98**
石鹼
AD—サンデザインアソシエーツ・辻本有邦
LD—板倉閲次
PD—中村明弘
C—牛乳石鹼共進社
1989

麝香（じゃこう）と白檀という2種類の香りをもつ石鹼だから，個装は思いきってエキゾチックなエスニック調。装飾性を備えたロゴタイプを，さりげなく上品にレイアウトした。百貨店での贈答品として売られることを念頭にした商品である。なによりも贈り主が満足感を味わえるよう配慮された高級感がある。ロゴタイプを縦向きにして石鹼本体に刻印したときの効果がすばらしい。

**98**
Soap
AD—Sun Design Associates, Arikuni Tsujimoto
LD—Etsuji Itakura
PD—Akihiro Nakamura
C—Cow Brand Soap Kyoshinsha Co., Ltd.
1989

This soap has two kinds of fragrances, musk and sandalwood. The package, with its decorative logo, is intentionally designed to look ethnic and exotic in an inconspicuous way. Sold as gift items, the noble design will push the product in department stores, and will give the customers satisfaction. The vertical version of the logo impressed on the surface of the soap looks great.

RANFUAN
FRAGRANCED SOAP

**99**
リップクリーム
AD, LD―門前武夫
PD―城出栄子
A―シマ・クリエイティブハウス
C―サンスター
1988

口紅，リップクリームのロゴタイプだから，もともとは小さく使われるものだ。フリーハンドの楕円の囲み，ブダルラインの英字と中黒の多用で装飾性を持たせ，小さければ小さいなりに，工夫を凝らして，可愛らしいものを作る努力がなされる。

**99**
Lip Cream
AD,LD—Takeo Kadomae
PD—Eiko Shirode
A—Sima Creative House
C—Sunstar Co., Ltd.
1988

Logo for lip sticks and lip balms are allowed only a little space. Using handwritten ellipses, English characters in doubled lines, and inserting dots between each character give this one a decorative appeal. The designer must have gone through great pains to create a cute and effective logo for such a small item.

**100**
きざみタバコ
D—木村 勝
C—日本たばこ産業
1986

きざみタバコを紙で巻いて，自分で巻タバコを作って吸う人のためのキットである。30g，50本分の紙が入っていると書いてある。暇があって趣味で楽しむ人たちのためにと，遊び心を盛り込んだ，装飾的なロゴタイプが作られた。商品の対象は若い人なのだろうが，筆者としては，昔，さんきらの葉を乾してきざみ，粗末な紙で巻いて吸っていた父のことを思い出す。45年も前のことだ。

**100**
Tobacco
D—Katsu Kimura
C—Japan Tobacco Inc.
1986

This is a hand rolled tobacco kit for people who enjoy rolling their own. It contains 30g of tobacco for making a total of 50 cigarettes. For people who have time to enjoy it, the logo was created to look snappy. Although the product seems to be intended for young people, it reminds me of my father's dried leaves, chopped and smoked with coarse papers 45 years ago.

STATS
SHAG CUT

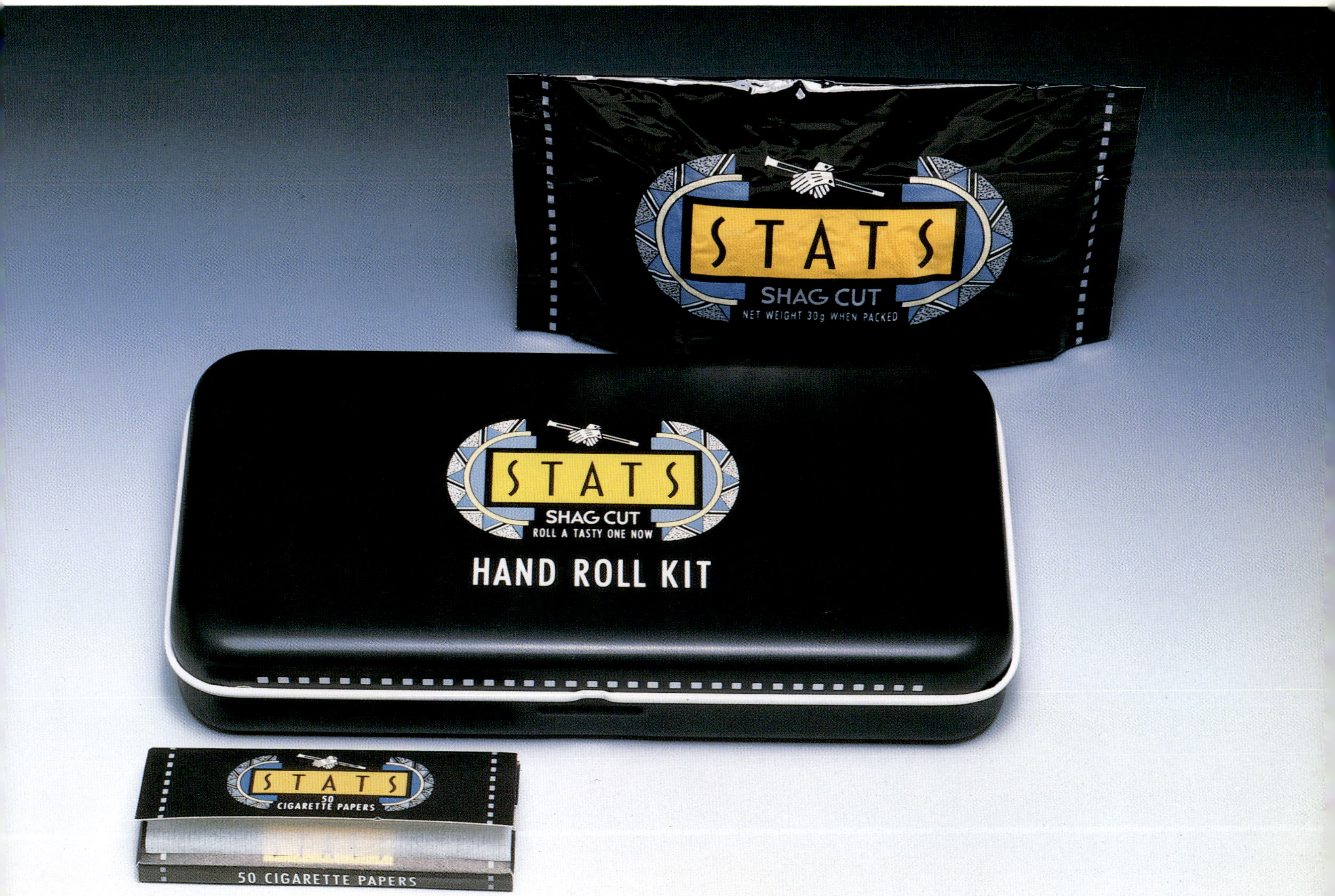

101
制汗剤・コロン
CD—渋谷紀昭
AD—吉川富士保
LD, PD—工藤雅子
C—大正製薬
1990

遊び心のデザインもここに極まった感がある。読める読めないの次元も超越してしまった。これはもうロゴピクチャーだ。(そんなことば聞いたことないが)だから敢えてここでは解読しない。
ソフトで清潔な感じの商品があふれるなか，これは強烈，ビビットカラーで押し切ってしまった。それぞれ香りがちがうようだけど，面白いからみな買って行っちゃおう——そんな効果を狙った〈EXIN〉である。

101
Deodorant, Cologne
CD—Toshiaki Shibuya
AD—Fujio Yoshikawa
LD, PD—Masako Kudo
C—Taisho Pharm. Co., Ltd.
1990

This is a logo to have fun. It's above considerations of whether it can be read or not. I would call it "Logopicture" (though I never heard the word). So, I would not bother reading it. Among the products which look soft and clean, this uses vivid colors and gives an energetic impression. They offer different kinds of fragrances and people might think to buy all of them simply because they are fun. That could be what the designer had in mind.

**102**
コンパクトディスク
D—染谷淳一
C—ポニーキャニオン
1988

コンパクトディスクのタイトルは，ロックとニューミュージックが面白い。ポニーキャニオンの〈GOBANIC LAND〉は女性3人のグループ，ゴーバンズのアルバムであるが，タイトルもアーチスト名も，想像力豊かで痛快なデザインである。技法はいわゆる切り文字だが，その手間のかかる作業にもかかわらず，自由奔放にデフォルメされたユーモラスでエネルギッシュな文字群が印象的だ。

**102**
Compact Disks
D—Junichi Someya
C—Pony Canyon
1988

Logos of compact disks in rock and pop music are exciting. Gobanic Land, an album manufactured by Pony Canyon, Inc. is played by Go' bans, a three-girl band. Logos for both the title and the name of the band are designed to look unique and thrilling. They are created by cut outs. Nevertheless, it is delicate hand work, the finish boldly deformed. These amusing, energetic letters are quite impressive.

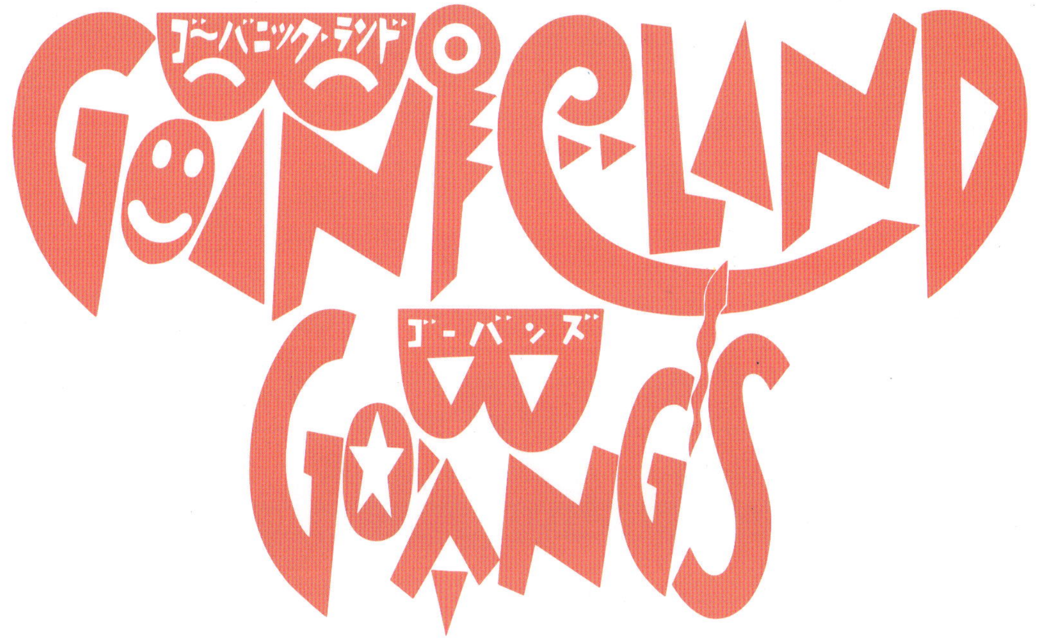

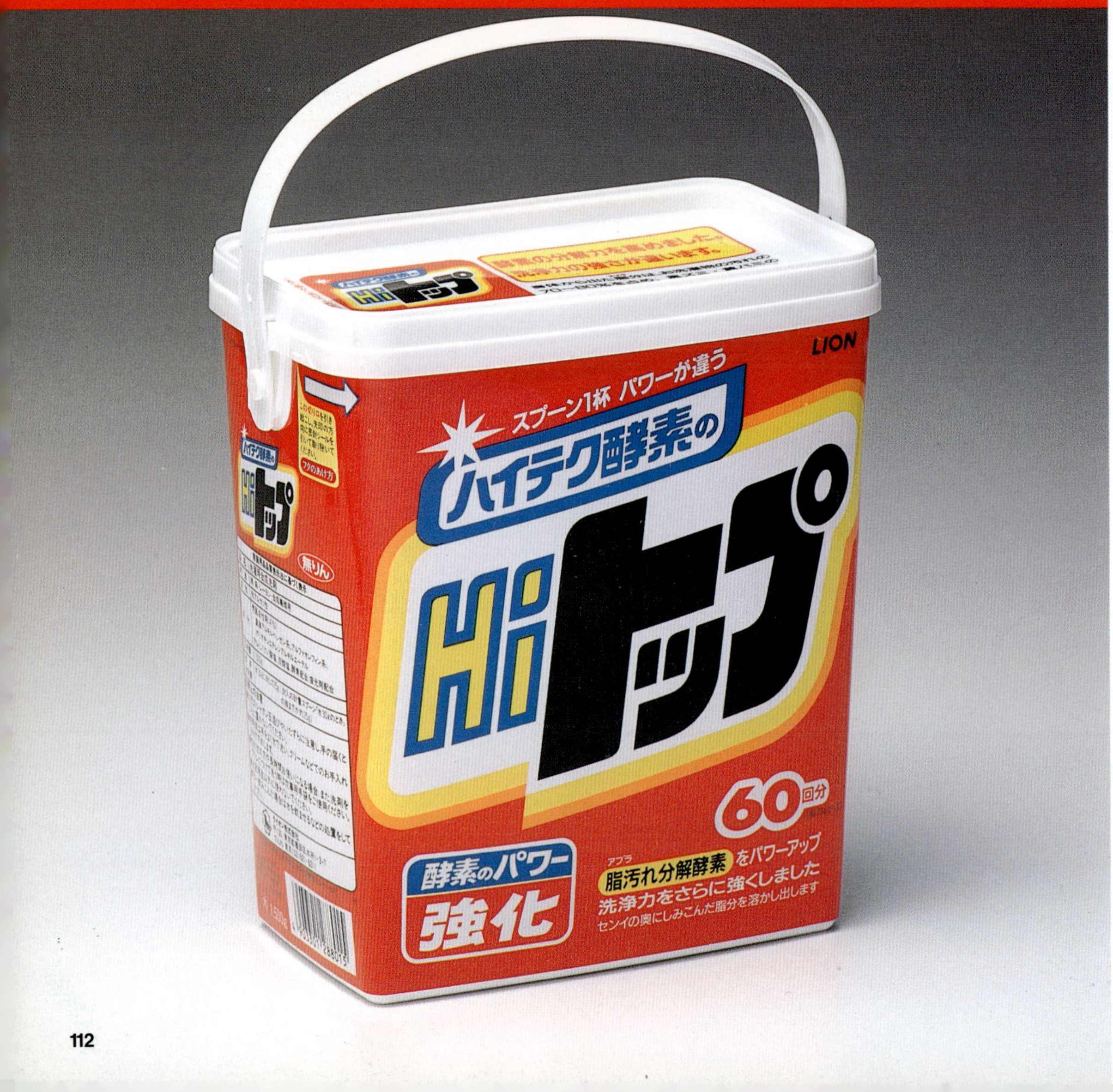


**103**
洗濯用洗剤
CD—岡田一朗
AD—吉光純也
LD—デザインマック・平山博之
PD—デザインマック・高野 清・吉光純也
C—ライオン
1988

英字商品があふれるなか，家庭用品だけは日本字が主流である。この分野の商品は毎日の消耗品であるだけにメーカー間の競争は激しく，勢い派手で，強烈で，声高なデザインになりがちである。性能や使い方も細かく記載しなければならない。パッケージをデザインする人たちの困難でつらい状況を想わないわけにはいかない。俗っぽい，品がないと言われながら，しかし，業界の長い間の努力で，それなりの，いや，この分野でしか作り得なかった様式感をうち立ててきたことを認めなければならないと思う。その優れた成果のひとつが，このライオンの〈Hiトップ〉ではないだろうか。
ツボを心得たレタリング，並みのパワーでは抗しきれない底力を感じさせるレイアウトと配色，ケースの構造や大きさも研究され尽したに違いない。

**103**
Laundry Detergent
CD—Ichiro Okada
AD—Junya Yoshimitsu
LD—Design MAC, Hiroyuki Hirayama
PD—Design MAC, Kiyoshi Takano, Junya Yoshimitsu
C—Lion Corporation
1988

The logos of most household goods still display Japanese letters now where the majority of other products embrace English letters. Since household goods are everyday products, the manufacturers are in keen competition. Thus the design of packages tend to be loud. Also, for household goods, it's necessary to explain how to use them and their specifications on the packages. One should recognize that the designers created the style of the design which could uniquely provide for household goods, while previous designs had been criticized for looking cheap or vulgar. A typical example of the attained designs is Lion's Hi Top. The lettering shows that they know what lies at the heart of the product. The color arrangement and the layout bring you to feel its power. Careful research must have gone into manufacturing a suitable size and shape for the package.

**104**
柔軟仕上げ剤
AD—井上憲之
D—永井 満
C　花王
1988

花王の家庭用品のロゴタイプは常に高い完成度と安定感があってひと目でそれとわかるデザインである。
太くて力強いが丸味を帯びて柔らかく，ブルーを基調にした色彩でいつも統一されていて，その清潔感が好ましい。この柔軟仕上げ剤ハミング1/3も例外ではない。1/3とはやわらか成分が濃縮されて使用量が従来の1/3に減ったという意味である。

**104**
Laundry Softner
AD—Noriyuki Inoue
D—Michiru Nagai
C—Kao Corporation
1988

The design of Kao's products can be recognized at a glance for their mature, balanced logos. The company's logo, sturdily structured and powerful in appearance on the one hand while producing a rounded, soft feeling on the other, centers on a color tone underlined by blue, and transmits a feeling of cleanliness. This also applies to its laundry softener, "Humming 1/3."

スプーン1杯で驚きの白さに

アタック

**105**
衣料用洗剤
AD—吉田光利
LD—井上憲之・永井 満
PD—青山明輝
C—花王
1988

〈アタック〉も花王の洗剤として一般によく親しまれているヒット商品である。ただし，成分が改善されたり用量に変動があるたびにパッケージもロゴタイプも少しずつ手直しされてきた。'88年にデザインされたものが現行商品であるが，濃いブルー，丸味を帯びた太いレタリングという花王の顔は常に堅持されている。

**105**
Laundry Detergent
AD—Mitsutoshi Yoshida
LD—Noriyuki Inoue, Mitsuru Nagai
PD—Akiteru Aoyama
C—Kao Corporation
1988

Attack is one of the popular detergents of Kao, which turned out to be a hit. The design of the package and the logo have been changed several times with improvements in the ingredients or changes in the capacity. The product now on sale was redesigned in 1988. It keeps the Kao feature of the design-rounded, bold lettering and deep blue for the background color.

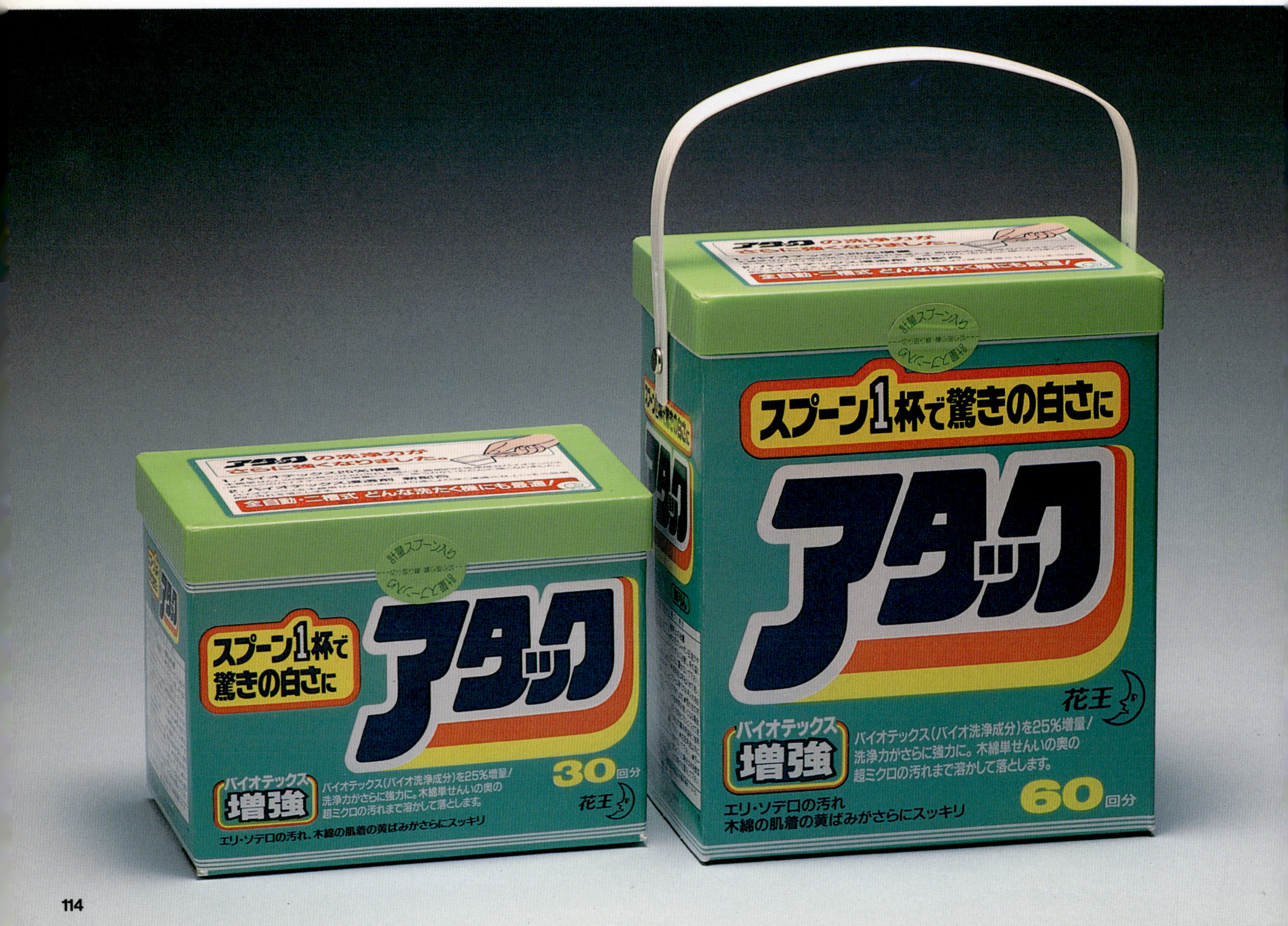

**106**
調味料
AD—河北秀也
D—明星秀隆・谷井郁美
A—読売広告社
C—桃屋
1989

桃屋から発売されたばかりの中華料理用調味料〈汎〉は，容器全体にわたって展開されたタイポグラフィワークの素晴らしさに，まず引きつけられる。ロゴタイプもその一部分としての位置と役割を持つことになり，決して大威張りすることはない。写植の書体だけをこれだけ積極的に使って，しかも美しく見せる力量は並みではない。汎は汎用性の意で，この5種類があればだいたいの中華料理はできるという。

**106**
Seasoning
AD—Hideya Kawakita
D—Hidetaka Myojo, Ikumi Tanii
A—Yomiko
C—Momoya Co., Ltd.
1989

The Chinese seasoning, Han, has been on sale only recently. The typographical work spread throughout the whole bottle looks good enough to attract customers. The logo maintains a position as just one element of the typography, and never stands out on its own. It is quite an achievement to make it look neat only using boldly constructed phototypes. Han got its name from the word "Hanyousei" which means "general purpose". They claim that you can cook most Chinese food using these five kinds.

MOMOYA

中華重宝調味料

汎

[fàn ファン]

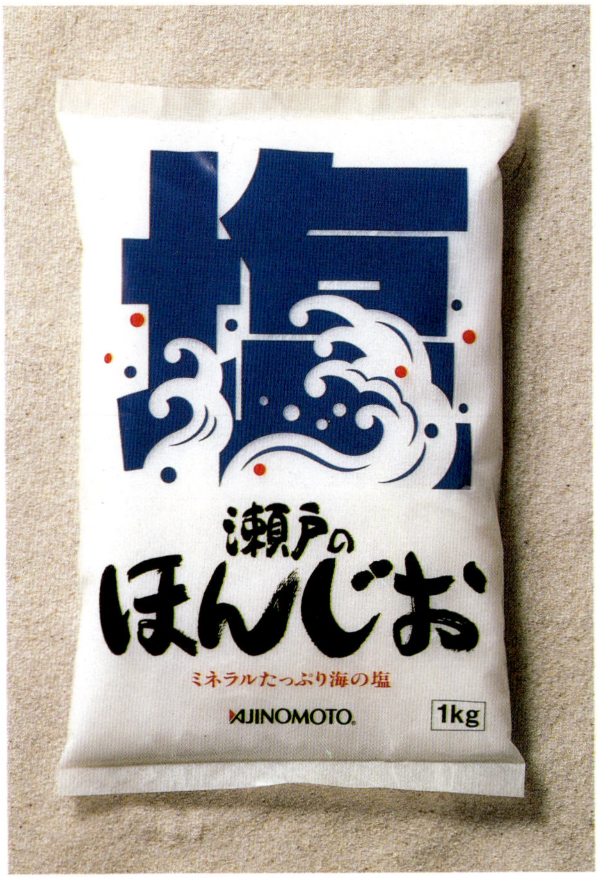


**107**
食品(塩)
CD—梅田悦史
AD—島崎紘而
LD—富田幽甫
PD—名久井貴信・中田淑子
C—味の素
1988

ひと頃，文字遊びというか，漢字のエレメントの一部分を絵にさしかえたり，花鳥風月を添えて，その感じを楽しむことが流行った。この〈塩〉の場合もそんな試みのひとつである。浮世絵や紋章の波のパターンを借用して，私たちはいつも海のイメージを共有することができる。超特太ゴシック体で字画に隙間がないから，白い波が砕ける様子をより鮮明に表現することができた。

**107**
Cooking Salt
CD—Etsufumi Umeda
AD—Koji Shimazaki
LD—Yuho Tomida
PD—Takanobu Nakui, Yoshiko Nakada
C—Ajinomoto Co., Ltd.
1988

Playing with letters, such as altering one element of a character in a drawing or expressing an image by adding the beauty of nature, has been popular at certain times. Here is one such example. We are always able to share an image of the sea by using wood block prints depicting worldly ways and a coat of arms. Since there is no space due to the large gothic style, breaking white waves could be expressed with clarity.

**108**
食品(さけフレーク)
AD—岡田宏三
D—岡田宏三・山岸武行
C—宮古水産加工業協同組合
1989

宮古市の水産事業の切り札として開発された，さけの加工食品のブランドである。宮古=みやこの語呂を生かして〈385さけ〉と命名された。「さけの宮古から，食卓の新スタンダードナンバー "385" という訳だ。写真にみる料理素材としてのフレークだけでなく，ご飯にのせて食べるもの，酒のつまみ，わさび漬，粕漬など多くの関連製品がある。
ヘルベチカ体+民友明朝体という正統的な文字組みにリアルなさけのイラストが加わって，博物誌的な魅力をもったロゴタイプである。

**108**
Salmon Flakes
AD—Kohzo Okada
D—Kohzo Okada, Takeyuki Yamagishi
C—Miyako Suisan Kakogyo Kyodo Kumiai
1989

This is a salmon processed food brand which has developed as the trump card of the marine products industry of Miyako City. Using the sound of MI·YA·KO (mi=3, ya=8, ko=5), this product was named "385 Sake." There are other products besides the flakes for the ingredients shown in the photo, such as products eaten with rice, a snack with a drink, Japanese horse radish preserved in sake lees, and fish pickled in sake lees. This logo presents an historical image, with orthodox characters arranged in Helvetica and Minyu Ming-cho type, and a realistic salmon illustration.

**109**
ラム酒
AD—佐野幸義
D—木村 功・原 伸子
I—松本秀実
A—東急エージェンシー・インターナショナル
C—キリン・シーグラム
1987

昔から船乗りはラム酒を飲んだものなのだろうか。
「船長がラム酒を飲んでゐる」
飲みながらなにか唄ってゐる
(略)
船長の胸も赤いラム酒の満潮になった
その流れの底に
今宵も入墨の錨が青くゆらいでゐる」
(丸山薫「錨」)
陽焼けした海図の上に，朽ちはじめた明朝体の〈漂流記〉。ながい冒険と漂流ののちに故国に生還した船長の航海日誌をひもときながら飲む酒である。

**109**
Rum
AD—Yukiyoshi Sano
D—Isao Kimura, Nobuko Hara
I—Hidemi Matsumoto
A—Tokyu Agency International
C—Kirin Seagram
1987

I wonder if sailors drank rum even in the old days?

"The captain's 'a drinkin' rum, and 'a drinkin' rum, i's a singin',
The captain's chest turned 'a high tide 'o rum in the depth of that flow,
Tonight, too, his tattoo's 'a swayin'."
——Kaoru Maruyama, "An Anchor"

This is a story of drifting laid out on a discolored map in decaying Ming-cho type letters.

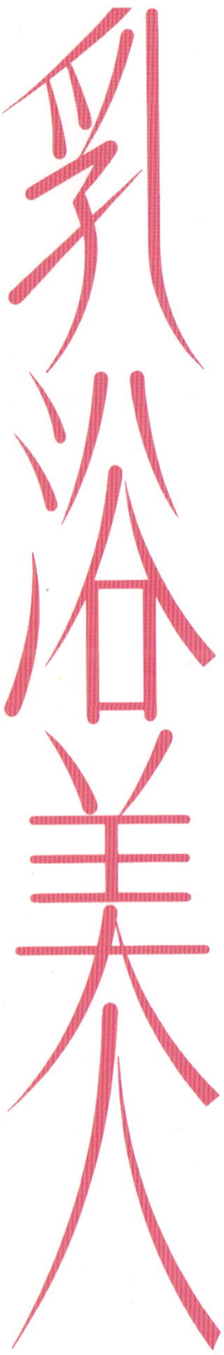

**110**
入浴用牛乳
D—平松 暁
C—キャピタルフーズ
1988

これは想像力をかきたてる作品だ。色白でほっそりした美女が，牛乳風呂に入ってお肌しっとり，ほんのり桜色みたいな情景が浮んでくるではないか。細く，あくまでも細くと，はやる力を抑えて書きあげた繊細な文字だ。パッケージの色も食品では考えられないようなまめかしさである。

**110**
Bathing Milk
D—Satoru Hiramatsu
C—Capital Foods Co., Ltd.
1988

This work stimulates one's imagination. One can imagine a slender, fair-skinned beautiful lady in a milk bath with cheeks flashing light pink. The lettering is thin and delicate and the coloring is unbelievably bewitching for a food package.

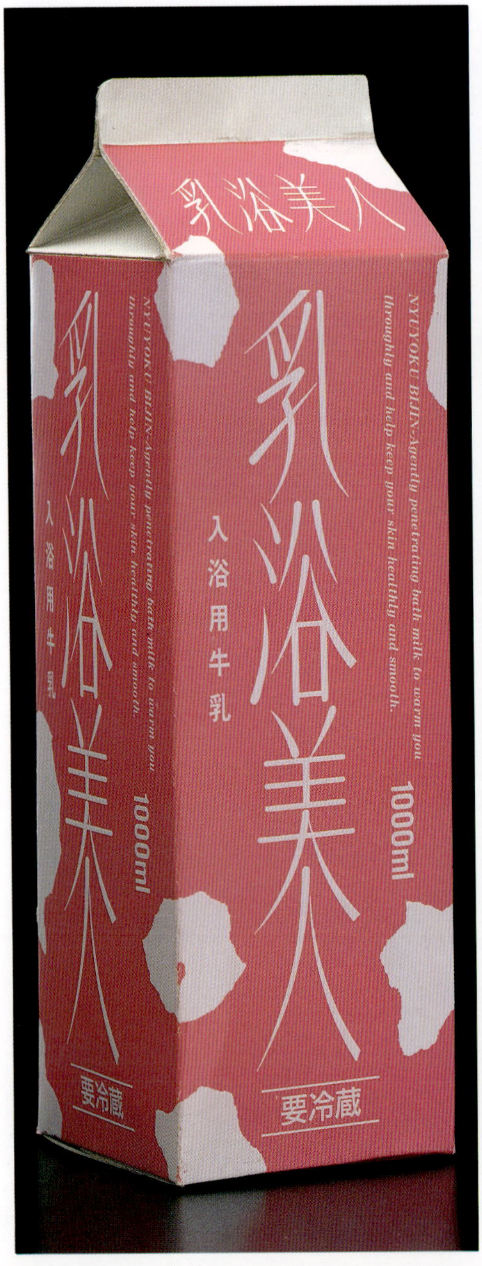

**111**
梅酒
AD—藤重日生
D—藤重日生・高橋好光
C—中国醸造
1989

漢字に花や果実のイラストを組み込んだデザインはよく見かけるが，しかし何度見ても楽しいものだ。果物のリアルなイラストは常に食欲をそそる。この〈梅酒〉はとりわけ大粒で美味しそうだ。深緑色のロゴタイプも中身の味の濃さが感じられてよい。

**111**
Plum Wine
AD—Teruo Fujishige
D—Teruo Fujishige, Yoshimitsu Takahashi
C—Chugoku Jozo Co., Ltd.
1989

One can always find designs in which the lettering is combined with fruits and flowers. This remains interesting regardless of how many times you view it. A real photo of fruit builds one's appetite. This plum wine filled with large plums is especially delicious. The dark green logo and the power of the flavor are easily felt.

**112**
ワイン
D—立松 脩
C—山梨薬研，甲斐醸造
1988

生産地の地名を冠した製品は，とかくその地の風光などを描いて情緒的，説明的になりがちだが，この〈勝沼〉はその手の技法を敢えてとらず，文字表現にのみ意を注いだ。
明朝体に突然荒っぽい筆を入れて普通であることを避け，見る者の注意力を喚起する。ドライな表現に徹して地場産品の匂いを払拭するのにも成功した。

**112**
Wine
D—Osamu Tatematsu
C—Yamanashi Yagen Co., Ltd,
Kaijyozo Co., Ltd.
1988

Products displaying the name of the place or origin are apt to draw the natural beauty of that place and tend to be sentimental and expository. KATUNUMA relies only on the lettering for its expression. This lettering avoids the common by its brusque, rough Ming-cho style and really catches the eye. It further succeeds by eliminating the odor of its local manufacture, focusing on a dry expression.

サッポロ生ビール

# 北海道

*Just as the best malts, hops, and other ingredients are native to the northern climes, so does the Northern Star shine on this custom-brewed, limited-run edition bringing you the bracing taste of Hokkaido's rustic flavor.*

**113**
ビール
AD—勝岡重夫
D—勝岡重夫・平出敏雄
C—サッポロビール
1990

〈冬物語〉に続いて出されたサッポロビールならではの好企画だ。
ロゴタイプにも，背景となるラベルや缶にも絶え間なく雪は吹きつけていつ止むとも知れない。これがアルミの地肌そのままに吹雪となっていたらどうだったか。あまりに描写がリアルで手が出なかっただろうとも思う。寒さに弱い人も手が出るようなホッとした暖かさがあって安心できる。その辺がデザインの妙というものだろう。

**113**
Beer
AD—Shigeo Katsuoka
D—Shigeo Katsuoka, Toshio Hiraide
C—Sapporo Breweries Ltd.
1990

This is a nice project following on the heels of "Winter Story" by Sapporo. Snow fall seemingly without end against the logo and the background of the label and can. What would happen were there to be a blizzard directly on the aluminum can? It would have been too realistic, out of reach. This design can reach even those easily affected by the cold, relaxing and warming them. Perhaps this is the peculiararity of this design.

**114**
清酒
CD, LD—U.G.サトー
PD—平良勝彦
C—吉久保酒造
1987

〈一品〉とはもちろん天下一品の意味。水戸で生まれて200年，常陸随一の清酒のブランド，そのスタンダード商品が写真でご覧に入れるものである。
ロゴタイプは髭文字の技法を最小限にとり入れて純化し，その簡潔な姿で，伝統よりもいまを生きている商品であることを強く感じさせてくれるデザインだ。あふれんばかりに咲き競う梅の花が，白抜きの文字を一層ひき立てている。

**114**
Sake
CD,LD—U.G. Sato
PD—Katsuhiko Taira
C—Yoshikubo Syuzo Co., Ltd.
1987

'Ippin' means, of course, 'the greatest.' Created 200 years ago in Mito, it is the best sake brand of the Hitachi area. This design, with its logo of slightly feathered lettering, by its concise appearance, makes us strongly feel that the product is more modern than traditional. Plum flowers in full bloom show off the white letters.

常陸銘酒
一品

**115**
清酒
AD, PD—武友正修
LD—武友朋子
C—世界一統
1987

“一”という字は縁起の良い文字として古今，最も多く使われてきた文字ではないだろうか。その名も世界一統という（大隈重信の命名），和歌山の酒造会社の清酒〈一〉（イチと呼ぶ）は，墨をたっぷりとふくませた筆でグイッと書き出してひと筆が終結する前の，あふれるような力感だけをズバッと切り取ってきたような，一種凄味さえ感じさせる佳作だ。漆のように光るキャップといい，渋さと品位を合わせ持ったラベルといい，ルックスだけで買ってきてしまいそうな魅力がある。

**115**
Sake
AD—Masanobu Taketomo
LD—Tomoko Taketomo
PD—Masanobu Taketomo
C—Sekai Itto Co., Ltd.
1987

'1' has always been the most frequently used 'auspicious' character. This sake is named, 'Sekai Itto' (named by Shigenobu Okuma). '1' from Wakayama Sake Breweries is written in colorful calligraphy, representing a vague dread. This product is attractive. The cap shines like lacquer and the label is cool and dignified.

**116**
即席めん
CD—高橋和廣
LD, PD—森永正広
CW—板東睦実
A—博報堂
C—明星食品
1989

となりのコンビニエンスストアで見つけた“一”は，ご存知明星ラーメンの〈味の一徹〉である。材料にも味にも徹底的にこだわって作るので〈一徹〉と名付けられた。筆文字仕上げの極太一文字に写植のゴナUを組み合せて，いかにも頑固一徹なヘビー級ロゴタイプになったのを，しょうゆ味は金色に，とんこつ味は赤い文字にして上手に逃げ，大衆性と市場性を獲得するデザインとなった。それぞれの味に袋とカップの2タイプあり，後で冷し中華とコーン味が加わった。

**116**
Instant Ramen
CD—Kazuhiro Takahashi
LD, PD—Masahiro Morinaga
CO—Mutsumi Bando
A—Hakuhodo Inc.
C—Myojo Foods Co., Ltd.
1989

The horizontal '1' represents the well-known ramen Aji no Ittetsu, named for the particular nature of its ingredients and taste. This logo achieves a stubborn, heavy image by combining a super thick '1' in brush stroke with typesetting Gona U. the design captures popular and market appeal by writing the 'Ittetsu' in gold for the soy sauce flavor and in red for the Tonkotsu flavor. There are 2 types of noodles, cup or packaged, for each flavor. Later, cold noodles and corn flavored were added.

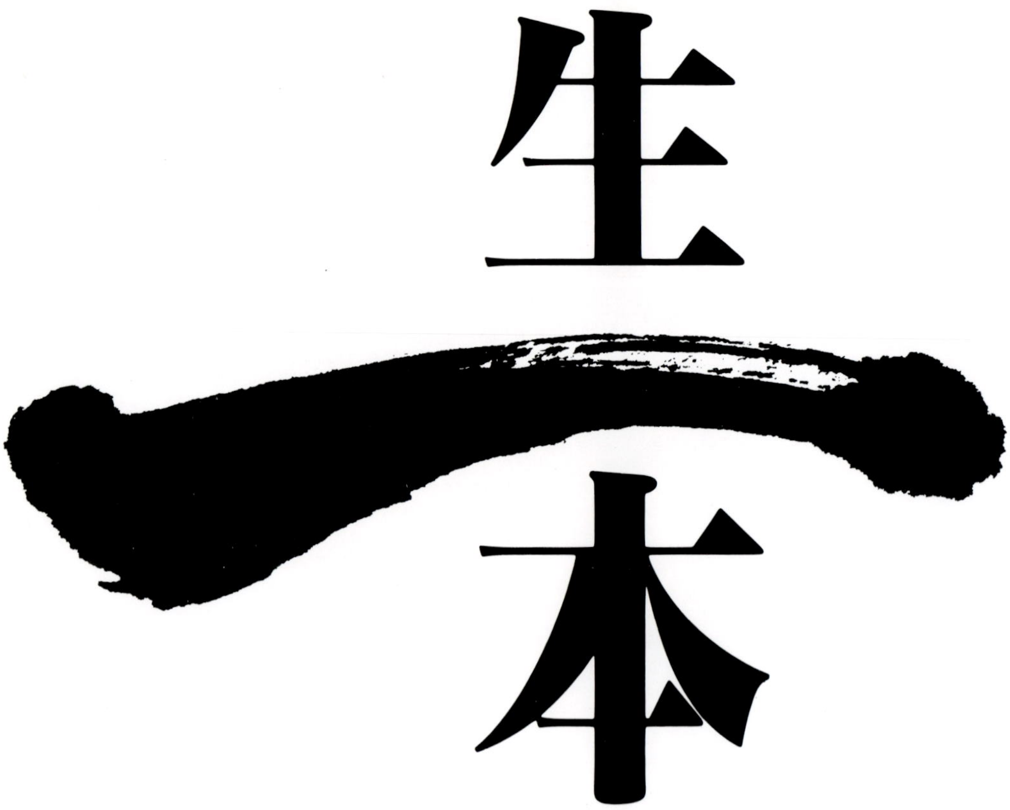


**117**
清酒
D—及川利春
C—あさ開
1987

北国岩手にも“一”がある。あさ開の清酒〈生一本〉は写植の大蘭明朝体との組み合わせである。書き出しに，ふくませた墨を使いきり，あとは勢いにまかせて書ききった満足感が伝わってくる。写真でお見せする〈純米酒〉も同じあさ開のシリーズ商品で，他に本醸造，辛口，樽酒とラインアップされている。ラベルもタイポグラフィのセンスが良く，清々しい仕上りである。

**117**
Sake
D—Toshiharu Oikawa
C—Asabiraki Co., Ltd.
1987

Asabiraki's refined sake, 'Ki Ippon,' is a combination of typesetting and Oran Ming-cho type. It speaks of the full use of ink in the expression of this one character, the horizontal '1.' The junmaishu, using only rice, in the photo is one of the same series. Others, junmaishu, dry, and barrelled are also available. The label's typographic is excellent and refreshing.

**118**
清酒
AD—U.G.サトー
LD—関 南沖
PD—平良勝彦
C—吉久保酒造
1988

これは正に“祝い酒”だ。きっかけは水戸市制100年を記念して発売された銘柄だが，私たちが〈百〉という字に託す思いを考えれば，今後いろいろな場で振舞われる有難い酒であり続けること必定である。書家の揮毫になるものだけに一味違った風格があり，それを大胆にも箱からはみ出すほどにズームアップして見せたので迫力は倍加した。これは先に紹介した〈一品〉の一銘柄である。

**118**
Sake
AD—U.G. Sato
LD—Nanchu Seki
PD—Katsuhiko Taira
C—Yoshikubo Syuzo Co., Ltd.
1988

This is certainly a sake drank at celebrations, the brand sold in honour of the 100th year anniversary of Mito city. Written by a calligrapher, this '100' has a slightly different flavor. Furthermore, it is larger than the box itself, increasing the impact even more. This is also an Ippin brand.

HIBIKI

**119**
ウイスキー
AD—横尾 浩
D—牛島志津子
LD—荻野丹雪
C—サントリー
1989

サントリー創業90年記念ウイスキーである。10年，20年の長期熟成モルトを幾種類もブレンドした，その豪華な〈響〉きをお楽しみください――という訳で，1本10,000円である。
ロゴタイプというより，書家による記念の揮毫をラベルに持ってきたといった印象。サントリーホールを中心に音楽事業に力を入れていることも，ネーミングのヒントになったかもしれない。

**119**
Whisky
AD—Hiroshi Yokoo
D—Shizuko Ushijima
LD—Tansetsu Ogino
C—Suntory Ltd.
1989

This is a 90-year-old Suntory whiskey. A blend of several kinds of malt ripened for 10 or 20 years, 'Hibiki' whiskey is justifiably priced at ¥10,000. The impression is one of a calligrapher's work more than that of a logo.

**120**
ビール
AD—大森重志
D—柳田美保
LD—荻野丹雪
C—サントリー
1989

サントリーではこのところ筆文字によるロゴタイプの商品が相次ぐ。左ページの〈響〉，そして〈山崎〉というウイスキーがあり，この〈冴〉だ。書は〈響〉と同じ作者だが，こちらは明らかにデザインとして楕円のラベルに使われることを意識して書かれたと思える，おさまりの良さがある。いや，おさまりが良いのはデザインが冴えているからだ，と反論があるかもしれないが。色は光沢のある赤金。冴えとは，のどごしとうまさが冴える——の意味であることは言を待たない。

**120**
Beer
AD—Shigeshi Omori
D—Miho Yanagida
LD—Tansetsu Ogino
C—Suntory Ltd.
1989

Nowadays, Suntory produces many logos for its products via brush-'Hibiki,' 'Yamazaki' whiskey and this 'Sae.' This was written by the same calligrapher as for Hibiki, but the oval of the label was a conscious effort and is well-balanced. Or rather, this clearness is due to the sharpness of the design, with its reddish-gold color.

**121**
清酒
AD—小川デザイン事務所
LD—鮎川静竹
PD—宇野たまこ
C—小堀酒造店
1988

酒のロゴタイプが続くので恐縮だが，もう一杯つきあっていただきたい。
先がすりきれるまで使い古したような筆でたどたどしく書いてあるように見えながら，黒白のバランスに十分神経を使って慎重に仕上げたことを感じさせる小堀酒造店(石川県)の〈純米〉。これも実は書家の手になるものだった。ラベルから化粧箱に至るまで一貫したアートディレクションのもとで作られた作品の，質の高さを示す良い例である。世に純米酒は数多いが，パッケージデザインの美しさなら，まずこれに指を折る。

**121**
Sake
AD—Ogawa Design Office
LD—Seichiku Ayukawa
PD—Tamako Uno
C—Kobori Sake Brewing Co., Ltd.
1988

This is a pure rice sake from Kobori Sake Brewing in Ishikawa prefecture. The lettering looks as if it is written with a very old, used brush. And yet, it makes us feel that enough consideration was put into the balance of black and white. This is also written by a calligrapher. From the label to the decorative box, high quality art direction is presented.

**122**
食品(いわし漬)
D—藤重日生
C—津田婦人会
1986

私たちは伝統の味，ふるさとの味，おふくろの味と言われると，一も二もなく手を出す。それらの商品の包装や箱を手がけるデザイナーも，伝統の味，ふるさとの味を表現する技術，技法に磨きをかけてきた。その研さんの成果を，この〈いわし漬〉に見る思いがする。
稚拙さを装った筆文字，版画や切り絵による民家，民具。ざら紙に印刷したような不鮮明な文章，そして茶色の和紙。なにもかもつぼを心得た人のなせる技だと感嘆する。

**122**
Pickled Sardines
D—Teruo Fujishige
C—Tsuda Fujinkai
1986

Designers who deal with traditional food products' wrapping and boxes have improved their techniques and skills. We see the results of their research in this 'Iwashizuke' (pickled sardines). The lettering is amateurish, like that of a private house, done block print or cut outs, unclear characters as if printed on rough paper and brown Japanese paper. All of these are skillfully executed.

DELICIOUS RICE CRACKER

KAKIYAMA

KAKIYAMA ORIGINAL ARARE OKAKI GIFT SET
PRODUCED BY KAKIYAMA CORPORATION

**123**
和菓子(米菓)
D—佐竹起造
C—柿山銘菓
1986

柿山の和菓子(米菓)はギフトセットが中心である。丁寧に包まれた1枚1枚，詰め合せの美しい化粧箱，いずれの場合もこのロゴタイプが，青金，灰色，茶灰色といった渋い色で展開される。渋い分だけ高級感も増す。
無造作に書きなぐったような筆文字だが，周囲を長方形に切り揃え，端正な英文を添えることで一挙にモダンなロゴタイプに変身した。

**123**
Japanese Confectionery (rice cakes)
D—Kizou Satake
C—Kakiyama Meika Co., Ltd.
1986

KAKIYAMA rice cakes are sold primarily as gift sets. Whether wrapped individually or in a decorative, this logo written in bluish gold, grey, and brownish grey sober colors. The soberer the colors, the greater the quality of feeling. The writing appears to be careless calligraphic writing, but, in fact, is quite a modern logo due to cutting the perimeter into a rectangle and including English.

**124**
食品(かまぼこ)
D—デザインルームP&P・真田 彬
C—まるなか本舗
1989

寿司屋の茶碗に書いてある魚偏の字を最後まで本気で読んだ人はいないだろう。たいていの人は，読めないから，どうせ当て字だからと逃げてしまうのではないだろうか。しかし，この“旬の彩”の場合はれっきとした長崎のかまぼこである。必ずや記された魚を主原料にしているはずだ。読んで味わってみなければ意味がない。左からいしもち，たい，えそ，下へ行っていか，はもである。この場合，筆文字以外は考えられないだろう。達筆である必要はない。くせというか，スタイルがそろっていればロゴタイプの要件を満たすことになる。

**124**
Fish paste
D—Design Room P&D, Akira Sanada
C—Marunakahonpo Co., Ltd.
1989

'Shun no irodori' is clearly a Nagasaki fish paste whose main ingredients are written on the package. Eating it without reading the package is meaningless. Only brush strokes are possible here. Skilful handwriting is not really necessary. If the style is appropriate, the logo is good.

**125**
レトルト食品
D―ほてい缶詰
C―ほてい缶詰
1988

ほてい缶詰のお手軽グルメ一人前シリーズはストアのレトルト食品売場のなかで異彩を放っている。黒いパッケージがずらっと並んでいるのも凄い。毛筆描きの円形シンボルが7色(7種類の品揃え)に変化して虹のよう。単純で明快，強い訴求力を発揮している。
画僧仙厓が筆で丸を描いて「これを食って茶を飲め」と言った話を思い出した。いまはさざえやいかを食べたかったら○印を探せばよい。

**125**
Pouch-packed Food
D—Hotei Canning Co., Ltd.
C—Hotei Canning Co., Ltd.
1988

Hotei's handy gourmet 1-person series is a somewhat different from other similar products in stores' pouch-packed food sections. Rows of lined up black packages catch the eye. There are 7 colored, brush-stroked circles representing 7 different types. They are simple and cheerful with high marketability.

**126**
薬用入浴剤
D—今井敏之
C—純ケミファー
1988

わが家で有名温泉の気分と効果が味わえるという趣向の薬用入浴剤が人気だ。登別から下っていって別府あたりまで，シリーズ商品だからデザインも統一されていて目を引くが，初めて買う人は，とりあえず3ヶ所ぐらいの湯を試してみようか，ということになる。
純ケミファーの"旅のゆ"シリーズは，写植の書体「勘亭流(けんじ勘亭)」を巧みにアレンジして，文字だけで見せるタイポグラフィ派である。

**126**
Medicated Bathing Products
D—Toshiyuki Imai
C—Jun Chemifer Ltd.
1988

Medicated bathing products which offer the effectiveness and popularity of a hot springs are popular at our home. Since this is series product from Noboribetsu down to Beppu, the design is unified and attractive. First-time buyers buy about 3 varieties just to try them out. Jun Chemifer's 'Tabi no yu' series skilfully arranges the typesetting of Kanteiryu.

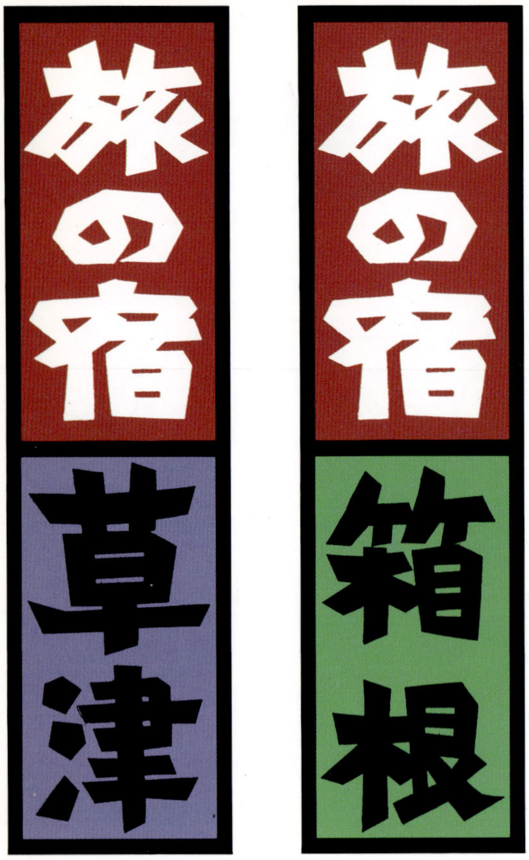

**127**
薬用入浴剤
CD—高橋平治郎
AD, PD—小林理恵
LD, I—木田安彦
A—第一企画
C—カネボウホームプロダクツ販売
1985

カネボウの温泉シリーズ〈旅の宿〉はイラスト派である。
切り文字によるロゴタイプ，それぞれの温泉の風物を描いた力強い版画，いずれも同じ作者の手になるものだけに表情に一体感があって印象は鮮烈。
後に“にごり湯”シリーズとして，十和田，奥飛騨，霧島の各温泉が加わり賑やかになった。

**127**
Medicated Bathing Products
CD—Heijiro Takahashi
AD, PD—Rie Kobayashi
LD, I—Yasuhiko Kida
A—Dai-ichi Kikaku Co., Ltd.
C—Kanebo Home Products Sales, Ltd.
1985

Kanebo's hot springs series, 'Tabi no yado,' is an illustrative series. The prints present strong images of scenery of each hot spring in cut out lettering and the impression is solid and consistent, for the illustrator is the same for all. Later, as the Nigoriyu series, the Towada, Okuhida, and Kirishima hot springs were added.

**128**
ワイン
D—木田安彦
C—サッポロビール
1986

異色かつ華麗なこのワインのラベルは，京都のワイン愛好家のために限定販売されたサッポロ・マイタウンワイン〈京シリーズ〉のものである。透き間なく黒々と書く日本の伝統文字の定石を守りつつ，それをのり越えた荒々しいまでに力強い切り文字の中に，色鮮やかに散りばめられた京の風物詩。いうまでもなく“嵐”は嵐山，“祇”は祇園，“西”は西陣…である。こんな魅力的なデザインのワインが京都向け限定販売とは何とも残念である。

**128**
Wine
D—Yasuhiko Kida
C—Sapporo Breweries Ltd.
1986

This unique and splendid wine's label was produced for the Sapporo My Town wine, sold in limited quantities. While keeping the traditional Japanese characters, this cut out lettering has exceeded them and represents the feeling of Kyoto. It goes without saying that 'Arashi' refers to Arashiyama, 'Gi' refers to Gion, and 'Nishi' to Nishijin.

**129**
食品（茶漬）
D—氏原忠夫
C—田丸屋本店
1988

芹澤銈介がきり開いた民芸の手法をデザインの分野で巧みに生かして，長い間活躍してきた氏原忠夫氏の仕事である。70歳を越えて，いまも元気に制作されていると聞く。
田丸屋の製品のパッケージは全て氏が担当する。文字と絵とが一体となって，懐かしさに満ちた手作りの味が届けられる。

**129**
Food (Ochazuke no moto: tastily seasoned dried food sprinkled over ochazuke, boiled rice with tea poured over it)
D—Tadao Ujihara
C—Tamaruya Honten Co., Ltd.
1988

This is the work of a Tadao Ujihara, active in the graphic design world using folkcraft work techniques developed by Keisuke Serizawa. All packaging designs of Tamaruya's products are designed by Mr. Ujihara. These logos represent the homemade taste, combining logo and illustration into one.

**130**
食品(漬物)
D—藤重日生
C—青水農産加工組合
1987

切り文字の魅力は，小刀の勢いが直線的，鋭角的に文字に残されること，元来が型染めから発した技法だけに，文字のエレメントがあちこちでつながっていることであろうか。その二つを踏まえつつ，素朴だけでは済まない文字の美しさを体得しているのが，この〈一本漬〉である。あとは墨刷りであろうと白抜きであろうとその魅力は少しも変らない。中国山地の一町村に，これだけのデザインを身につけた農産品があるのだ。

**130**
Japanese Pickles
D—Teruo Fujishige
C—Aomizu Nosan Kako Kumiai
1987

One of the attractions of logos using cut outs is that you can distinguish the sharpness from the work on the logo. Another is the connection of letters, for the technique derives from cut and dye. The logos of 'Ipponzuke' are designed to show these two elements. Using either white or black letters is attractive.

**131**
清酒
AD—Y工房
D—溝渕浩治
C—福寿酒造
1990

レタリングを独学で練習していたころは新聞の初号活字を拡大して，きれいに修正して再現することが唯一の教材だった。いつの頃からか，小さな印刷文字を拡大して，インクで字画がつぶれた様子やかすれたところが，かえって面白いんだとされるようになっていた。
福寿酒造の〈夢ごよみ〉，やはり味わいがある。輪郭が定かでないところに夢の儚さが出ている。白いボトルの白い文字を見ていると静かにまどろむ心地さえする。

**131**
Sake
AD—Y Kobo
D—Koji Mizobuchi
K—Fukuju Shuzo Co., Ltd.
1990

Fukuju Shuzo's 'Yumegoyomi' gives you a tasteful impression. The unclear outline evokes an evanescent feeling of dreams, as if dozing off while looking at the white letters on the white bottles.

132
清涼飲料(甘酒)
D—鈴木 進
C—森永製菓
1983

これはどう見ても花祭りの甘茶の気分だ。ならば甘酒の気分とはどんなものか。ビニールの袋に入った乳白色の液体。それではまるで糊だ。いいじゃないか，どうせ楽しく美味しく飲んでもらうんだ，花祭り結構。桜の花の満開の下で飲む甘酒，そんなデザインでいこう。
以後，私たちは甘酒と聞けば，赤い花模様の森永〈甘酒〉を思い浮かべることになった。

132
Soft Drinks (Amazake—a sweet alcoholic drink made from fermented rice)
D—Susumu Suzuki
C—Morinaga & Co., Ltd.
1983

You can see the feeling of a flower festival on the cans. What then, is the feeling of the beverage? If it is that of being packed in a clear plastic bag, it would be the look of starch. Thus, the design has been made to resemble a beverage drunk under cherry blossoms.

**133**
コーヒー飲料
D—カンパニースタイル
C—ダイドードリンコ
1990

切り文字，切り絵は伝統表現ばかりがお得意様ではない。コミックだって，ほらご覧の通り料理してみせますよ。
調子がよくて軽っぽいけど，写植やインレタでカッコ良く済ませてしまうより，熱意がこもっていて好感がもてる。1字1字切っていった人が，楽しみながら仕事をしていた様子がわかるようだ。

**133**
Coffee
D—Company Style, Inc.
C—DyDo Drinco, Inc.
1990

Cut outs admit not only the traditional, but suit funny looking logos as well. They can illustrate the positive effects of handwork.

**134**
コンパクトディスク
D—染谷淳一
C—東芝EMI
1988

アイドルからロックに転身して自分のバンドWILD　CATSと作ったアルバムMINAKO with WILD CATSとその中から2曲とり出したCDシングル〈あなたと熱帯〉，とくに後者は切り文字の技法の制約を難なく乗り越え，イマジネーションのままにナイフが動いていった，そんな軽さとスピード感を見ることができる。写真中央は17cmEPレコード。この3枚のディスクがマゼンタ＋モノクローム写真というシンプルなデザインで共通しているのも心憎い。

**134**
Compact Disks
D—Junichi Someya
C—Toshiba-EMI Ltd.
1988

Here we have 2 CDs, the album and the single of Minako with WILD CATS. The logo of the single shows the sense of the speed of a moving knife, the same rhythm as the image of the music. The 17 cm EP record is in the center with a sophisticated look using a common design with a monochrome picture in magenta only.

**135**
健康飲料
AD—岡崎美保
D—奥村昭夫
C—サントリー
1988

これは中国北魏の碑の拓本である，というと本気にする人がいるかも知れない。中国に昔から伝わる珍しい薬草のエキスを程良く配合した飲料で，愛飲すれば身体の健康を保つ。その効きめたるや七賢人を上回るから〈八仙人〉と名付けたと筆者は推理する。
碑文と見紛う文字は写植の“淡古印”体のアレンジ，烏龍茶に盛んに使われているが，こちらの方が役者が一枚上だ。

**135**
Nutrient Drinks
AD—Miho Okazaki
D—Akio Okumura
C—Suntory Ltd.
1988

This is a compound of rare herbs from ancient China. The logo is the arrangement of the Tankoin type in phototypes. This type is popularly used for the logos of oolong teas.

**136**
食品(かつおパック)
AD—大丸デザインオフィス
LD, PD—松岡和明
C—大丸
1988

百貨店の大丸(大阪)のオリジナル食品,かつおパックシリーズに共通して使われるロゴタイプである。
これも石碑の拓本を思わせて,文字の欠けた状態や墨ののらない様子などを細かく演出している。書体も古い時代(そのままか分らないが)の印影を用いて歴史を感じさせ,老舗の特選品であるというところまでイメージをつないでいる訳だ。

**136**
Katsuo pack - packed dried bonito shavings
AD—Daimaru Design Office
D—Kazuaki Matsuoka
C—The Daimaru, Inc.
1988

These logos are commonly used throughout the original Katsuo pack series by Daimaru department store in Osaka. They resemble a rubbed copy of letters on stone monuments, representing the details of blurred or chipped letters. They evoke a feeling for the good ole' days and further represent the image that they are a prized item of a long-established department store.

**137**
紙おむつ
AD—村 武史
D—鈴木良彦・森近恵子・秋吉喜久子
A—電通EYE
C—ネピア
1989

ティッシュペーパーでお馴染みのネピアの紙おむつ。少し小さい子と発育のいい子ではお尻の大きさも違うから，赤ちゃんの世界にもSサイズ，Mサイズ，Lサイズがある訳だ。可愛いお尻から膝，足首にかけての丸々とした柔らかい感触が，そのまま〈ドレミ〉の文字に表われていてほほえましい。ロゴタイプの背後にある，まゆの形をした色のスペースも，もちろんおむつの形状を案じたものであろう。

**137**
Paper Diapers
AD—Takeshi Mura
D—Yoshihiko Suzuki, Keiko Morichika, Kikuko Akiyoshi
A—Dentsu EYE
C—Nepia Co., Ltd.
1989

This logo looks heartwarming as it represents the soft sense of a baby's lower body. The outlined background colors represent a form of a diaper.

# INDEX

## クライアント

五十音順　数字は作品番号を示す。



## 作家・代理店

五十音順　数字は作品番号を示す。
代理店もこの欄に掲載してある。

# ロゴ ON パッケージ

編者略歴——**長谷川純雄**

1939年名古屋生れ
愛知学芸大学(現愛知教育大学)美術科卒業
長谷川デザイン研究室主宰
162 東京都新宿区原町3-62 三佳ビル403号
TEL03-202-5545
編書＝「資料/マーク・シンボル・ロゴタイプ」シリーズを「1973→75」年版より7冊,
「同/カラー篇①,②,③」
「歌舞伎勘亭流」(以上グラフィック社刊)
日本タイポグラフィ協会会員

**Sumiwo Hasegawa**
Born in Nagoya in 1939.
Majored in Art at Aichi University of Education.
Member of Japan Typography Association

Other published works:
*A Collection of Trademarks and Logotypes in Japan* series - 7 volumes
*Japan's Trademarks and Logotypes in Full Color* series - 3 volumes
*Kabuki Kanteiryu* (compilation of characters used in kabuki)
All works published by Graphic-sha Publishing Co., Ltd.

翻訳———ウイン・コーポレーション
English Translation : WIN Corporation

発行日———1990年8月25日　初版第1刷発行

編者———長谷川純雄©
発行者———久世利郎
印刷所———凸版印刷株式会社
製本所———和田製本株式会社
写植印字——三和写真工芸株式会社
発行所———株式会社グラフィック社
102 東京都千代田区九段北1-9-12
TEL03-263-4318　振替東京3-114345
落丁, 乱丁はお取替え致します。

ISBN4-7661-0548-6 C3070 P3980E